PHILOSOPHICAL FRAGMENTS
1909-1914
and
THE PHILOSOPHER AND PEACE

Gabriel Marcel

PHILOSOPHICAL FRAGMENTS

1904-1914

and

THE PHILOSOPHER AND PEACE

Introduction
by
LIONEL A. BLAIN

UNIVERSITY OF NOTRE DAME PRESS—1965

The original French title of this book is
Fragments Philosophiques, 1909-1914
published in 1961 by
Éditions Nauwelaerts, Louvain
English translation by Lionel A. Blain

Editor's Note

In this book we are presenting the earliest formal philosophic reflections of a man whose distinguished career has extended over the first half of this century. It seemed appropriate to us to preface these early meditations with those given but recently on the occasion of the presentation to Gabriel Marcel of the Peace Prize of the Börsenverein des Deutschen Buchhandels *on September 20, 1964, at Frankfurt am Main. The topic of M. Marcel was one that is of importance to all of us, peace among the nations of the world. The peculiar position of the philosopher as a spokesman for humanity is broached, and the problems of his position are related in terms that can be appreciated by the reader living in our society of complex allegiances and commitments.*

Gabriel Marcel

The Philosopher and Peace

Ladies and Gentlemen:

First of all I wish to express my deepest gratitude to those who have done me the great honor of awarding me the Peace Prize. I must confess that I am very happy to receive it.

It would please me to believe that my work, the significance and value of which is subject to my constant scrutiny the nearer I approach the end, might have contributed something, be it ever so little, to the cause of peace, which, in my opinion, is by far the most precious of accomplishments. It is not sufficient to say that peace is a good; one must contend that it is the basic condition for everything truly good. I believe that all of us today must repudiate with disgust the thought that war possesses its own peculiar fertility. The use of destructive weapons, which we have experienced with horror and despair, has at least made it quite clear that war is something fundamentally evil, and this in contradiction of the pronouncements, if not by Hegel and Nietzsche themselves, of a great number of their disciples.

7

As it almost always happens to me at the beginning of such an examination, my attention has been directed toward certain paradoxes giving cause for thought.

One such paradox which occurs to me might be stated in this manner: while, on the one hand, peace appears to be the essential element in any existence worthy of the name, it also seems to be one which we cannot discuss without getting lost in the worst kind of platitudes. What is the reason for this? Does one have to reply that peace is in its essence something quite simple which, therefore, can be comprehended not through analysis, but rather through purely rhetorical enthusiasm? Let us be careful; the concept of simplicity contains a dangerous double meaning. There is, of course, the elementary simplicity which in its existence does not seem free of doubts for us but constitutes the presupposition of each synthesis. However, it is quite obvious that when traditional theology, rightly or wrongly, insists God is a simple concept, we are dealing with quite a different simplicity, a simplicity in which all differences are united, blended, and overcome. Yet, we must recognize how easy it is to confuse these two, in reality, opposite forms of simplicity, and it is this confusion of which the ideologists become guilty almost without exception.

Now what do I mean in this context by an ideologist in contrast to a philosopher in the true sense? An ideologist is an intellectual who lets himself be imprisoned in a web of pure abstractions. An example will clarify my idea: the thought of equality—if one disregards its purely mathematical application—can only mislead the ideologist. Never could a philosopher who deserves the name take seriously the thought of equality in its application to human beings. He can see only a μετάβασις ἐις ελλο γένος, an inadmissable transference, since human beings, regarded per se, give no cause for a thought process which bestows sense to the concept of equality. To say that human beings are equal is just as unreasonable as to desire their becoming so (which, by the way, also makes no sense whatsoever). On the contrary, it is desirable to establish an order in which *each* being would possess a certain superiority over others. But even this kind of proposition is open to criticism because such a formula again includes comparisons, and it is especially the temptation to compare that one must resist. Therefore, let us speak rather of a brotherly world, where everyone can enjoy finding qualities in his brothers he does not possess himself.

From here we return straightway to our topic, for with complete justification one could say exactly of such a brotherly world that it is at *peace*, while a world where general equality is demanded and claimed is incapable of this for a reason which under examination becomes evident at once: assuming that what one calls equality could be accomplished somewhere, it would inevitably be questioned again, for each of the equals would inevitably try to rise above the others. This would be a condition of constant tension which is not compatible with what we call peace. This tension will sub-

side in me, however, after I have learned to appreciate the
values which I recognize in others, knowing that I am want-
ing in them.

Nevertheless, we must recognize that this brotherly world
presupposes a certain identity—I do not say equality—of
fundamental rights, that is, of what could be described as
the fundamental conditions of social existence. How could
a brotherly world be possible where the utmost want meets
with conspicuously flaunted affluence? Owing to an easily
proven fallacy, one mistakes the identity of the fundamental
rights with the equality of the individuals to whom these
rights are not conceded but adjudged.

Introducing the concept "brotherly world" into this context, I hope to point out at the same time how each one of
us, no matter how modest his position and how limited his
horizon, can contribute to the work of peace.

Yet, will it not be held against me that I evade the crucial
problem of political order? We want to know if, in the field
of *politics*, an *engagement* of the philosopher in favor of
peace is feasible and how it can or must be understood. It
seems to me that here one has to avoid a double trap. In
the first instance, the philosopher is approached all too frequently by the demand that he get himself involved, that
is, make apodictic judgments about some concrete situation
of which, in reality, he has rather incomplete knowledge.
Many of us have been called upon to lend our signatures
to this appeal or that petition, mostly drawn by people

caught up in purely political ideas. Here I speak from experience and must confess that I myself have often failed from weakness and the fear I might be thought conservative, indifferent, or unfeeling if I did not sign, although I undoubtedly should not have permitted myself to care about these possible reactions. Experience shows, unfortunately, that these petitions, even when they are completely justifiable, hardly achieve anything, and that by giving one's signature one tries above all to obtain a clear conscience.

There is still another trap. It can happen that the philosopher rejects becoming engaged, not from cowardice, but because to him everything political seems essentially impure. I believe that therein can lie an error at least equally as grave as that of which I just spoke, an error which is doubtlessly based on the image of purity. Abstaining *per se* is assuredly not pure, be it only for its ambiguity and for the reason that he who abstains cannot be quite sure of his real motivations.

The only solution satisfactory to me is to distinguish as carefully as possible between the cases in which universal principles are at stake, where by abstaining one would consequently become the guilty participant in an inexcusable blunder, and the decidedly different cases involving questions of pure opportunity. Let me offer an example: on the day of the recognition of the government of Communist China by France, I was asked to sign a protest recalling the crimes ascribed to the Peking regime. Yet it is only too evident that other long-since-recognized Communistic nations can be charged with similar crimes. Furthermore, in principle, it is bound to appear absurd to deny the existence of a nation of 600 million people. Consequently the only question is one of opportunity; if the moment of recognition has been chosen well or badly. This is a difficult and important question on which, in my opinion however, the philosopher, as such, is not equipped to take a reasonable position, that is, by force of rationally decisive arguments. I therefore regarded it as my duty to refuse my signature, although by disposition I was inclined to give it.

I emphasize again that the philosopher must of necessity guard against the temptation to believe that his name on a piece of paper could change something, whatever it may be; and this for the reason that he, as a philosopher, knows the snares into which the ego inevitably falls when it remains self-satisfied.

Does this not amount to stating that, in matters of politics, where everything is decided, the philosopher has to admit not only his incapability but even his complete incompetence? To so contend would be going too far. Still, which role can one assign him when the object is the preservation of peace? I believe that the word *watchman* characterizes his role most accurately. By this term I understand "watch" as meaning to stay awake, or still more exactly, to fight against sleep in oneself. But with what kind of sleep are we dealing? Sleep can manifest itself in diverse forms. First, there is indifference, the feeling that I cannot achieve anything, a fatalism which, by the way, can take on different aspects. From it also originates the comfortable optimism of those who think that things will arrange themselves in the long run (as if events had not strikingly repudiated this kind of confidence). At the same time there is the voluntary nonparticipation of those who, using the excuse that everybody is lying anyway, neither read newspapers nor listen to radio. To keep awake means to react actively against everything that could induce acceptance of this cowardly or indolent attitude. Certainly there is a virtue of watchfulness the philosopher has to practice within the framework of the possible. But this must be directed, I believe, above all against every kind of propaganda and especially that of which the public powers make almost incessant use, even in countries not subject to dictatorship. One can without hesitancy state in principle that all propaganda, no matter how it is conditioned, works in the interest of war to the same degree that it contributes to incite one group against another, even without intending to do so. I want to add that, no matter how paradoxical this assertion may sound, it also includes pacifistic propaganda. History reveals all too frequently how unconsciously it works in the interest of the propaganda of the opposition.

In this regard, however, several questions emerge: If the philosopher practices this watchfulness solely for his own benefit, what purpose does it then serve? Which positive value can one ascribe to it? On the other hand, how could one hope to win the press, conditioned as it is in most countries, to the service of a militant clear-sightedness, inherently free of all group and party interests, a press which has as its goal the establishment of peace?

Experience shows, convincingly enough, that the difficulties involved are not merely theoretical. The power of money —a poor power, to be sure—always has to be called upon in order to arouse public opinion; to bring to its consciousness the threats which, in a given moment, burden the fate of the country and even the whole human race, because whatsoever happens in one corner of this planet today, whether one likes it or not, is bound to affect life even in the most remote countries.

It is indeed tragic that there are always people whose second thoughts are suspect, who try to turn to their own advantage appeals born solely of good will; and the philosopher is not always clear-sighted enough—he is, generally speaking, too harmless—to notice in which way his idea may be exploited by people who have nothing in common with him. That this is so is painful but perhaps inevitable, for if the philosopher had a more penetrating vision he would possibly lose his courage and sink back into scepticism.

It is by no means my intention to underestimate the various difficulties encountered by the person who, today, in this threatened world which surrounds us, tries to fight for peace. I think of neither exclusively nor principally external difficulties, but rather of the insoluble contradictions with which he is confronted in his own mind if he is honest. I would have the feeling of being dishonest if I did not admit to an uncertainty in this situation, or a perplexity from which I have not yet succeeded in finding a way out. In spite of its indisputable merit, even the voluminous book Karl Jaspers has dedicated to this problem doubtlessly does not aid in solving a difficulty rooted so deeply in our situation.

On the one hand, I must believe that it is not justifiable in itself to take refuge in nuclear weapons. As a Christian I am convinced that this infringes upon a command I have to regard as absolute. On the other hand, as a responsible writer, I do not accept for myself the right to advocate unilateral disarmament which, circumstances permitting, could deliver the free world, without possible recourse, to the attacks of an opponent to whom conscience is merely a word without content. I remember, after discussing this problem with students at Harvard University, encountering a completely justifiable anxiety in regard to this tremendously serious question. No aspect of this alternative may be excluded or underestimated. It seems to me one can only hope to gain time under these prevailing conditions, so that on the other side reason has a chance to succeed gradually against an ideological fanaticism which leads to war on its own accord. However, the word *reason* is perhaps not too well chosen here. It is difficult to believe that a philosophy of enlightenment such as Lessing's, whatever its moral value may have been, could once more rule a world so deeply affected by despair. Rather, we can count on a revival of Christianity, at least in those countries etched, perhaps indelibly, by the spirit of Christ. For China, things are different, and here the problem is as frightening as possible. Even in regard to Eastern Europe a most delicate question is posed. Actually the question is, At what price can one preserve what is called "gained time"; with what concessions must one pay? Under no circumstances should the price be so conditioned as to dangerously weaken the position we want to defend. The vision of the artichoke, gradually, piece by piece, stripped of its leaves, appears at the front of our consciousness with all the horrifying thought associations with which it is burdened. Therefore, for the statesman the objective must be to develop a capacity for appraisal directed not only to the moment but, at least to the same degree, to the sometimes distant consequences of momentary decisions. I am convinced that here the philosopher has to become aware of his handicap. It would be evidence of the most insane delusion if he wanted to believe that he could replace the statesman, be it only in his imagination. He cannot do this any more than he could take the place of the surgeon. The responsibilities are very similar. In either case, one has to act at the right time, neither too early nor too late; an error in judgment of the *Kairos*, the golden irretrievable moment, can result in the most catastrophic consequences for all humanity. We have experienced such consequences at our expense and the expense of the whole human race.

May I apologize for advancing to the brim of an historical abyss from which, it seems, both our nations finally have risen in a way resembling a miracle. Actually, I do not care for the word *miracle* in this connection. To use it is to overlook in an inexcusable way the obstinate and quiet effort of so many courageous men who have suffered and fought in order to prepare the dawn of an era of friendship between France and Germany.

I hope you will forgive me for reminding you at this moment of one among them, one of the best, one of the noblest, Robert Schuman. I did not know him well, yet well enough to think of him today with emotion and gratitude. To him I dedicate my inadequate words.

The name Robert Schuman seems all the more fitting since it permits me to return to my initial topic of the brotherly world. He was one of those infinitely rare human beings who have proven by their example that a statesman, with the inevitably inadequate means at his disposal, nevertheless can work for the initiation of this community of hearts and spirits, the only legitimate goal one can set for history, even though this goal is inherently a suprahistorical one. Peace is, without doubt, an eschatological concept, yet each of us has to work for it—and how much more pertinent this becomes for those who govern us—as though peace could be attained tomorrow, as though it could be established within the framework of this mortal world.

Before I close I would like to speak more directly than

I have up to now of the true dimension, the metaphysical dimension, on which peace truly rests. For me, music has provided admission to this dimension since early childhood, and while I was working on this speech and once again heard the sublime quartet, Op. 135 by Beethoven, in the most beautiful theater in the world, I became aware that I had to remember, with all the gratitude with which he inspired me, the incomparable genius whose work offers to us the burning testimony of a soul which, having gone through the most desperate battles, found peace beyond the most insoluble tensions. This is the peace of a finite brotherly world. But one must add that it is neither forced upon us, nor, to be exact, acquired. No, it rises like a reviving breeze at the end of a hot day to him who has erred much and fought much, often against himself. Here Goethe's unique sentence, which unfortunately has become a commonplace for high school students, "Over all mountain-tops is quiet now," reveals its true sense. What indeed is a summit but a place where this breeze from somewhere, like a blessing from another world, touches the feverish brow of the hero? I know I shall never be able to express exactly and emphatically enough what these last works of Beethoven have meant to me. His "Missa Solemnis" is, for me, the masterpiece of masterpieces. Each time I hear it I feel as though it creates a vacuum around me. Of course this is only a delusion against which I have to defend myself, for the Highest excludes nothing; He embraces everything; and if He sometimes destroys what appears to be a glowing illusion ascending from nothingness, even that is only an act of compassion.

If there is a concept in my work dominating all others, it is without doubt that of hope, understood as *mysterium*, a concept, as I have previously stated, that is enlivened as though from within through ardent anticipation. "I hope for us of You," I have written, and that is still today the only formulation which satisfies me.

We can say still more accurately, I hope for You, Who are the living peace, and for us, who are still fighting with ourselves and each other, that one day it will be granted us to enter You and share your completeness.

With this wish and prayer may I conclude my reflections.

Translated by Viola Herms Drath

PHILOSOPHICAL FRAGMENTS
1909-1914

Foreword

Father Blain has asked me to write a few lines of in-troduction to these philosophical fragments, which date from before the war of 1914 and which, at the time, I certainly did not intend for publication. Thus I have had to reread these pages which I only vaguely remembered. I must admit that this reading aroused in me a kind of painful astonishment. I find it hard to understand today how, during the years immediately following the reception of my aggregation degree, and even after having had the privilege of hearing Henri Bergson at the College de France, I could still feel the need to undertake a groping inquiry pursued in such a rarefied atmosphere and with the help of tools borrowed from post-Kantian philosophy. Bradley—I had read *Appearance and Reality*—should have helped me shake off the strait jacket in which my thought was so tightly bound. Surely, I aspired with my whole being to be emancipated from it, but how badly equipped I was to effect this needed escape! If the war had not come along to overthrow the world which still held me prisoner, how long would I have continued to mark time in this way? That is the question I ask myself; it is not only insoluble, but also may not have any meaning.

Certainly, in the light of all that has followed, this inquiry, which suggests to me the laborious digging of an insect or of a mole, takes on a very precise meaning. At certain moments, it is as if it opened up on the sky, but only for a few moments, for example, when I denounce the error that is so common among the Idealists and which consists in making an object out of the subject and in converting it thereby into a sterile form. It is absolutely certain that in the most awkward fashion I, who then knew nothing about Kierkegaard, was tirelessly trying to discover that living subjectivity which, for the Danish thinker, was like a fountain of youth, the fruits of which, however, were not to be fully experienced until our own time.

But how desert-like were my approaches at that time! Surely, to understand the work taking place within me then, one must complement the reading of these *juvenilia* with that of the first two plays written at the same period, that is, *Grace* and *The Sand Palace*. Through a kind of economy that was rather singular and not at all deliberate, everything took place as if I were saving for drama the concrete insights which, in my philosophical writings, are covered over by a kind of veil. It must be constantly kept in mind that these were for me nothing but work notes designed to clear the way for a later creation.

But I readily grant that the publication of these notes can be useful to those who have made a serious study of my *Metaphysical Journal.* It should also simplify the task of retracing the genesis of this philosophical undertaking without isolating particular aspects of it.

Gabriel Marcel
of the Institute.

Introduction

FATHER ROGER TROISFONTAINES, IN HIS BOOK *De l'Existence à l'Etre*, was the first to make known the early unpublished work of Gabriel Marcel, which he classified in his bibliography and used in his analyses. After him, other authors, including Pierre Bagot in his book, *Connaissance et Amour: Essai sur la philosophie de Gabriel Marcel*, drew material from these unpublished writings. Monsieur Marcel himself has often referred to them in his conferences and essays.

These facts were bound to arouse the interest of M. Marcel's readers and to make them ask: When are we going to have a chance to read these writings for ourselves?

In the meantime the author of this introduction had begun to prepare a doctoral dissertation at Louvain on the problem of God as it presents itself in the early works of M. Marcel.[1a] He went to see M. Marcel in Paris, who gave him

[1a] *The Notion of Proof for God's Existence in the Early Writings of Gabriel Marcel*, typed doctoral dissertation, Institut Supérieur de Philosphie, Catholic University of Louvain, Louvain, 1959.

27

permission to examine his unpublished notebooks and who kindly helped him to transcribe a few. The result of these efforts was an appendix to the doctoral dissertation, which contained a kind of pre-edition of the texts appearing in the present book.[1b] After the defense of the dissertation a number of professors of the University of Louvain expressed the desire that M. Marcel authorize the publication of these texts. A request was sent to M. Marcel and he graciously consented. This is how this volume was born.

A few technical remarks will aid in an understanding of Father Troisfontaines' listing as "manuscripts," numbered I to XXIII, a certain group of unpublished writings that either antedated or were contemporaneous with the *Metaphysical Journal*.[1c] The texts of the present edition were chosen from among these "manuscripts," and the same numbering has been followed. Manuscripts I to XI inclusive make up the first group, the notes either antedating Marcel's immediate plans for a thesis or having nothing directly to do with this work. Manuscripts XII to XXIII, which constitute the second group, are notes for the thesis.

In this edition will be found extracts from manuscript IX

[1b] The principle guiding the selection of the texts to be included in the appendix (and hence in this volume) was their relevance to the problem of proving God's existence or, to put it more existentially, to the problem of attaining certitude concerning the reality of God.

[1c] Cf. *De l'Existence à l'Etre*, II, 422-23.

and all of manuscripts XII, XIV, and XVIII. Manuscript IX consists of four notebooks, each containing about sixty pages: (1) an orange notebook including (a) a short philosophical journal with entries dated from June, 1909, to May, 1910; (b) "Notes on the Theory of the Concept in Aristotle according to Hamelin"; and (c) notes on a "Theory of Reasoning"; (2) a gray notebook containing (a) notes on a play and (b) notes entitled "On the Metaphysical Ground of Value Judgments"; (3) a pink notebook containing (a) notes on Bradley; and (b) other philosophical notes; (4) finally a blue notebook containing (a) "Notes on Consciousness and the Ego" and (b) "Notes on the Theoretical Postulates of Religious Sociology." In the present edition the short philosophical journal of the orange notebook (1a, above) is the only part of this manuscript that has been included. While reading these excerpts, it would be good to remember that Marcel wrote these notes during his last year at the Sorbonne, the year leading to his *agrégation*. He was under the influence of the Idealists; but already, one senses that he is heading for his emancipation, witness his vigorous critique of their exaggerated intellectualism.

Manuscript XII is a green notebook of sixty pages, entitled *Reflections on the Idea of Absolute Knowledge and on the Participation of Thought in Being, Winter 1910-1911*. Here is a greatly unified work, the central thesis of which comprises an internal critique of the notion of *Absolute Knowledge*, a critique leading to the first outlines of a theory of

participation. This document is the result of the thinking
Marcel did during the year of rest he had to take after the
months of overwork preparatory to taking his degree. Young
Marcel spent time on the French coast as well as in Switzer-
land and began at that time to reflect seriously on his thesis.
The notes in manuscript XII are his first notes for this work.
It should be remembered that in March and April of 1911
Marcel wrote *Grace* (a play published in 1914 along with
The Sand Palace in *The Invisible Threshold*), in which he
treats the themes of faith and participation in a more existential manner. Manuscript XII serves as a theoretical
support for this play and throws much light on it. It seems
that Olivier, a man of good will and believing in the faith of
his brother-in-law without being able to accept the reality of
the object of this belief, is young Marcel himself, who, at
that time, was wrestling with the problem of God and of
the justification of Faith.

Manuscript XIV is a gray notebook of about thirty pages
bearing no title except the date *1912-1913*. It consists of
three unequal sections: (1) notes on the ground of values
(pages 1 to 11); (2) "Notes on the Problem of Immortality"
(pages 17 to 29); (3) notes on truth and the unverifiable
(pages 29 to 32). In this document Marcel tries to show
how the dynamism of dialectical reasoning is a thirst for
individuality and freedom, that only a free affirmation makes
it possible to pass to reality, and how love leads to belief in
the personal immortality of the self and in that of other

selves. The article published by Marcel in the special September issue of the *Revue de Metaphysique et de Morale*, 1912, is probably prior to this notebook and serves as background for it. After having taught philosophy in a *lycée* in Vendôme during the scholastic year of 1911-1912, Marcel did not return to that post in the fall of 1912. He was at leisure to pursue his research during the second half of 1912 and in 1913.

In manuscript XVIII, a pink notebook, twenty-two pages long, and entitled *Theory of Participation, 1913-1914,* Marcel attempts to show what dynamic link exists between the self as act and freedom, love and faith. Related to this notebook are the play, *The Sand Palace* (written in August and September of 1913), the first part of the *Metaphysical Journal* (from January 1 to May 8, 1914), and five other notebooks, that is, manuscripts XIX, XX, XXI, XXII, and XXIII, which constitute a first draft of the beginning of Marcel's thesis on religious intelligibility (in which the author tries to justify his choice of this subject and makes a critical review of the intellectualist and fideist positions).

The publication of these texts will make the early life and thought of Marcel better known. While accentuating the diversity of levels at which the thought of this great man evolved during his long and fruitful philosophical career, it will bring out as well the deep unity which has inspired it and will allow the reader to take another step forward on the road leading to the original sense-giving experience which is the inaccessible hearth and source of whatever is valid in a concrete philosophy like that of Gabriel Marcel.

FATHER LIONEL A. BLAIN
Our Lady of Providence Seminary
Warwick, Rhode Island, U.S.A.

Table of Contents

I

Excerpts from
First Philosophical Notes and Sketches, 1909 to 1914

[*Manuscript IX*]

June 22, 1909. This morning, quite by myself, it seems, I became aware of the eternal truth which alone can ground ethics; I knew this truth, but I had not lived it. The ego is only a negation, and we attain absolute thought only by becoming aware of the nothingness of our individuality: thus Hegel and Schopenhauer meet. No doubt this individuality is an expression of absolute thought; but insofar as it is a particular determination, it constitutes a pure and simple negation of that thought. The role of the first post-Kantians has been to extend the idea of Spinoza, which finds expression in the *omnis determination est negatio*, to the totality of what is objective. But our ego, our empirical existence, our very consciousness, whether we want it to or not, falls within this objective world; our individuality falls within the totality of our representations, and it has no more value or meaning than

35

they do. Nothing *is* outside the eternal subjectivity; and while writing this, I have already lost the intuition which carried me above myself a few moments ago. . . . The synthesis in us of a nature and of this absolute consciousness, of this supraconsciousness, is, as Coleridge understood it so well, the eternal mystery which religion attempts to solve. If life has a meaning, it can surely be only this: reducing whatever is nature in us to being the willed and conscious expression of that eternal thought; outside of this, no morality. . . .

"*Man kann sich überzeugt halten, und es ist* Pflicht *überzeugt zu sein, dass alles Unsittliche auch an sich und in seiner Wurzel schon unverständig ist, und umgekehrt gerade das, was der höchste Verstand erkennt, seinem innersten Wesen nach sittlich und mit allen sittlichen Forderungen übereinstimmend sein muss.*" (*Schelling,* Philosophy of Revelation, *Lesson 10, Nos. II and III.*)

July 4.　In spite of our efforts the problem of divine transcendence inevitably arises; whatever we might feel, it does not seem possible for intellectualism to succeed in grounding the reality of God in a broadened and dynamic conception of individuality. In intellectualism God never exists but for the philosopher; yet this is exactly what we do not want, for a purely philosophical religion could not be true. But one might point out that the affirmation of God is implied in every moral act, and not only in the awareness that we might have of our rational eternity. We would not wish to deny it. Yet the fact is that this implication remains obscure and that it is doubtful that we can be content with the obscure presentiment that we are acting in accordance with true reality. The objections of Schelling against the theory of Fichte remain valid, I believe. What then? Are we faced with the mortal leap of Jacobi? Must we resign ourselves to admitting that God is above reason and that reason reaches him only by repudiating itself? One thing is sure: first, that religion can only be grounded subjectively and then that it implies, at least as an essential condition, the abdication of what is individual. The role of the philosopher consists in teaching us, as all the great thinkers have done, the basic unreality of what we are accustomed to consider our nature. We are not really what we believe we are. But why this illusion, why these appearances? Here, we must admit, philosophy cannot help us any more. Between the rational nature which reflection discovers in us and the phenomenal reality which we attribute to ourselves, a reality which is neither more nor less illusory than that of the outside world, an abyss remains which philosophy cannot succeed in bridging. I realize, as I write these lines, how shocking they must be to the ordinary mind and especially to a "scientific" mind. "Listen," one might object, "we are what the world, what the infinite ensemble of laws which govern it, have made of us." Always the invincible equivocation: the belief in the somehow phenomenal existence of the rational order which we project on reality. Far from understanding that the laws of evolution are only conditions of intelligibility, people want to see in them existential structures, not realizing that they are guilty thus of the worst excesses of a transcendent providentialism, of the very thing they believe to have done away with. There is meaning in things only because the mind exists; this is a definitively established truth against which pseudo-common sense rebels in vain. The invincible difficulty which philosophy faces is the impossibility of deducing the finite. Why are we finite? Why are we finite beings? All metaphysics, it seems to me, fails to explain this essential fact. To deny the finite, as Spinoza tried to do, is too clearly to say nothing and to ignore the problem instead of solving it. To affirm that it could be explained by an infinite analysis (Leibniz), or to see in it a moment in an eternal dialectic (Hegel) which we find it impossible to reconstruct, is to presuppose what is being questioned. Why this infinite analysis? Why this impossibility? Here we reach agnosticism, the inevitable limit of a subjectivism which is aware of its own weakness.

July 6. The world is only thinkable through the form of rational necessity; on the other hand, it is only knowable through an experience which inevitably leaves much room to the contingent. And thus the problem of the contingent takes on a new aspect. Contingency, although it cannot be said to be at the root of things, is the expression of what is individual in reality; it is the clearest manifestation of the essential fact which metaphysics seems to have failed to explain until now and which is precisely individual experience; this is a problem which Kant, if he ever faced it at all, did not resolve. Passing from the universality of reason to individual experience is one of the most difficult and perilous tasks. It is quite possible that Fichte thought he had solved this problem; still, I must say that I cannot fully accept his doctrine on this point. At a certain moment in its development the absolute ego posits the individual ego; but why does it become individualized in such and such a way? We cannot explain it from the point of view of the finite; and, in any case, from the point of view of reason we must admit certain particular characteristics of the absolute ego (repugnant to what I call the universality of reason) which would make it posit itself in such and such a determined way. Whatever we might try to do, the last word of Fichteism is agnosticism. There is no transition from the infinite to the finite, as Brunschvicg saw so clearly after so many others. From the point of view of the infinite, the finite is negated as existence; from the point of view of the finite, the infinite is negated as knowable. What then?

Must we accept Fichte's thesis, all the while bringing it nearer to phenomenalism and eliminating from it what remains of Spinoza's doctrine? Must we call upon an intuition, religious or otherwise, to explain what, from the point of view of reason, seems to be an insoluble enigma? *I do not know.*

May 23, 1910. The given presents itself as contingent with regard to the intelligible form or the pure subject of reflection. But neither of these two terms is conceivable without reference to the other; the one and the other are limits of two inverse developments. However, the idea which posits itself first as pure finality, as an undetermined limit, becomes a law; and the contradiction inherent in any kind of realism of science consists in the fact that a law is likened to the given which it determines and is itself treated like the given. But we cannot be satisfied with these two abstract terms, an intelligible form and the contingent datum related to it; the truth lies in the act which brings them together to confront one with the other. This act is the mind; thus the relation of mind to experience turns out to be essentially different from what most of the philosophers of the past have thought it to be. If the mind can posit the ideal and the real in their reciprocal correlation, it is because the mind is not distinct from them, because they are the mind itself, because somehow they are the fixation of what makes up its essence. Experience is inherent in the very nature of the mind; experience is possible only in relation to a finality which gives it an orientation. As long as we take the word in a broad sense, we can say that experience is the mind itself exercising its activity.

May 28. I firmly believe that scientific truth is in no sense—
not even in the most rigorously critical sense—the measure of the real. On the other hand, it is not true to say that science is only an empty formalism; rather, it is such only if we arbitrarily isolate scientific findings from the spiritual activity which has engendered them. Science is relative to the spiritual activity which produces it, and it is a fallacy to see in the world considered as reified science a whole sufficient unto itself; for this science, as the great Rationalists realized, would demand a universal mind which would transcend it and make it possible. Completed knowledge would never be anything but an abstraction; it can only be conceived as an ideal related to working, living thought. However, who knows if we can posit even this mind in itself without falling into analogous contradictions?

II

Thoughts on the Idea of Absolute Knowledge and on the Participation of Thought in Being
Winter, 1910-1911

[Manuscript XII]

Can reality be conceived as absolute knowledge, as an intelligible system which would include in its concrete and individual unity all the particular elements of knowledge? Every intellectualism, it would seem, tends toward a conclusion of this kind; and, if critical exigencies sometimes intervene to limit the scope of the conclusions of intellectualism, it still seems to tend toward affirming the identity of being and knowledge. Is this notion of absolute knowledge coherent, is it free of all ambiguity and contradiction? Such is the problem which we want to take up.

It is clear that the problem of absolute knowledge is also that of the relations between the infinite and the finite. Absolute knowledge is infinite in this sense that it encounters no external limit; for this limit would be for it a pure datum, something abstract and not susceptible to being assimilated —in a word, something which could not be integrated in it: this is the same as saying that absolute knowledge would cease being absolute.[2] We could admit, if we wanted to, that another way of saying that absolute knowledge is internally infinite is to say that it is inexhaustible; or, better, that inexhaustibility is only the subjective stamp of the infinite, the expression of the effort made by discursive thought to embrace the intuitive totality of the real. But there is only one step from this interpretation to the following affirmation: to posit the infinite as inexhaustible is to translate an essentially positive characteristic in a negative and contradictory way. The infinite is transcendent with regard to

[2] We could make the allegation that knowledge would only cease being absolute if the limit-element was presupposed as ultimately knowable. This could be denied, it seems; knowledge as such can be absolute in that it covers everything that is knowable, and yet be transcended by a level absolutely beyond the grasp of knowledge. This objection, we believe, cannot stand up to analysis, for if this "level" is unknowable in the absolute sense, it simply is not as far as knowledge is concerned, and consequently it cannot limit this knowledge; the relation between the limited and the limit can well have meaning within knowledge, but not when the totality of knowledge is envisioned. And it is this very thing that is meant by the notion of infinity taken positively: not a movement beyond all limits (this movement only causing the contradiction to run on ahead, as Hegel saw, but not eliminating it), but a reality in relation to which all limits can only be posited as interior; the infinite is absolute positiveness, that is, it is nothing posited in a determined way; it is the real foundation of all affirmations. The question remains of knowing if this real foundation is anything besides a level of ideal possibility; we are not for the moment looking at the problem under this aspect.

any analysis. But is this not the same thing as saying that any conception that is finite (and progressive, the two characteristics implying each other) is false and contradictory to the extent to which it translates pure positiveness into negative language? To say that the infinite is beyond discursive thought is to say that *discursive thought, or again, that the finite simply is not*. To deny this would be to see in the finite an element of the infinite, while the infinite is manifestly beyond all composition; it would be to say that the finite is an element of what does not have elements. This contradictory formula brings out the difficulty exactly: the moment we posit the finite as real in any sense whatever, by that very fact we negate the infinite; the infinite cannot be reconciled with a method of juxtaposition. Thus intellectualism is led by an apparently invincible logic to negate the finite *as such*. In other words, if there is anything real in the finite, it will be the infinite; it is from the infinite that the finite gets the little reality it possesses; by itself, it is nothing, nothing but an abstract and contradictory view. No one has seen better than Hegel this absolute demand of intellectualism. Moreover, we can perceive easily that what is true from the standpoint of Spinoza's substance must also be true from the standpoint of absolute knowledge.

Hence, absolute knowledge seems to be infinite and to negate the finite as such. On the other hand, it obviously embraces and includes all that is real in the latter; it leaves aside, it excludes only negation. And a critical analyst of this language has no right to see a contradiction here: the infinite excludes the negations—but it is not exterior to them (how could *nothing* be exterior to something?), it goes beyond them. Absolute knowledge encompasses within itself the truth of all finite bodies of knowledge, which, as such, are irresistably destined to contradiction. The truth of the finite is in the infinite; and if this truth is presented to us by a neo-Hegelian like Bradley, as the end result of a method of infinite supplementation, we must not forget that this method is infested with contradictions and cannot be anything but an indefinite approximation of the real. This method leads to the strange result that the finite is an element of the absolute system, provided it is transformed. But the absurdity of this result is evident: no series of additions can make of an element anything more than an element; and, anyway, there do not exist any elements of absolute knowledge, there is no passage from the finite to the infinite.[3] Absolute knowledge, we have said, is an infinite system, but only if we avoid admitting that there are systematized elements. The elements exist only for minds that have partial and abstract conceptions of reality, and in those cases it is the systematization (conceived as concrete and absolute) which disappears. Here again, if the finite exists,

[3] We are well aware that, in one sense, thought is this passage itself, but it is an eternal passage, an eternal mediation—a mediation that is unable, so to speak, to renounce itself; and this is explained by the fact that it could not renounce itself without becoming an obstacle that would itself be overcome by that mediation.

the infinite does not; and then if the finite loses all its reality, all support, it negates itself. Affirming and negating the finite are identical acts; the difference between them is *Meinung*, as Hegel says. The infinite is not an abstraction, as too quick a judgment would risk making us think, but that in relation to which all is abstraction. The criterion of abstraction cannot be an abstraction; and that criterion is exactly what absolute knowledge is. One can see how partial truths might appear to be more or less perfect imitations of this pure totality, but these imitations cannot be anything but shadows. Even though light can produce shadows, the shadows are nothing without light.

Let us ask ourselves now what we mean when we speak of the concrete richness of absolute knowledge. We cannot be talking about specifications inside the absolute; the absolute, insofar as it is itself, does not admit of details. The details are always relative to finite and abstract conceptions; to speak of the concrete richness of the absolute is to say that the latter lends itself to an infinite multiplicity of abstract conceptions. It is evident in any case that this multiplicity can only appear as a criterion in virtue of an illusion; there is no criterion of a criterion when the latter is, itself, absolutely primary.

But let us ask ourselves in what sense one can speak about the universal comprehension of absolute knowledge. This knowledge cannot have a purely negative bearing. And on the other hand, unless we delude ourselves with words, we cannot see how we can avoid bringing in this unlimited possibility of abstract views, of finite thoughts, of experiences. One might reply that these abstract views are all relative to the absolute which is then independent by right and does not imply them. But here, as we see it, is how the question arises: by right it is possible that the absolute be conceivable without these partial views being brought in; but in this case the absolute is reduced to a pure affirmation, one which loses its quality of intelligibility. Intelligibility consists in a unity of determinations which are separable in the abstract, but it implies that these determinations subsist as such at the very heart of the unity; if they disappear, we are then dealing with some abstract and substantial identity. Absolute knowledge, then, is intelligible only if we think of the distinctions of the finite as subsisting in it, only if we do not abstract from the possible partial views. Yet thus conceived, absolute knowledge does not rest entirely on itself any more; it allows finite thoughts to be introduced *for which* it exists—in other words, it ceases to be absolute. We could formulate our conclusion as follows: absolute knowledge is intelligible only insofar as it is related to finite thought; but it is then exterior to it in a certain way; it is not absolute knowledge any more. There seems to be only one way of avoiding this contradiction, and it is obviously ruinous. It would consist in resolutely denying that absolute knowledge is intelligible; intelligibility, one could say, is valid within absolute knowledge, but not in relation to that knowledge taken globally. But this would be the same as saying that if we assume the intelligible systematization of the real to be completed, the intelligible disappears. In other words, intellectualism, when pushed to its outer limits, destroys itself. When we hypostatize intelligibility into an absolute system, we destroy it. If reality is this systematization thought of as complete, it is clear that reality is not intelligible; it is much too obvious that we shall not resolve this difficulty by saying that reality is *more than intelligible*.

Before further specifying what is to be understood by the identity of the intelligible and the real, before specifying the limits within which this notion appears valid, we must point out another difficulty to which we have already alluded.

Let us admit, although it is surely false, that the ambiguity of the notion of absolute knowledge can be dispelled, that we can, from the point of view of the absolute itself, speak of its concrete content. Still we are obliged to acknowledge that, if this concrete content is ideally identical with the content of all finite experiences, it cannot be posited except as the result of a transformation. The nature of this transformation is easy to understand in the abstract. It consists in uniting whatever is positive in finite thought and experience, while abstracting from the rest. This method, which seems clear at the start, becomes obscure upon reflection. The reason is that the use made here of the concept of negation is not clear. If we are dealing with an absolute negation, we do not see how it is possible not to set it aside. To set aside nothingness is obviously to leave things the way they are. If, on the contrary, we are dealing with a negation that is real—that is, determined— it seems much more difficult to set it aside. For this specified negation must correspond in the absolute to some affirmation (no matter how inaccessible it is to us), and then the method becomes complicated; we might add that it loses in clarity what it gains in complexity. But let us take one more step forward, although it is perhaps an ungrateful task to insist on a method which no one has ever been able to apply and which by definition is inapplicable by a finite mind.[4] Basically, it is a matter of abstracting from the external limits which are a condition of the reality of any finite object and have made of it a pure appearance. Without bringing up the question (which absolute Idealism, itself, declares to be insoluble) of the possibility of these limits, let us ask ourselves only whether absolute knowledge will not be a singularly fragmentary knowledge, a compendium obviously full of *lacunae*, an abstract summary of the real. And if we repeat that the limits cannot positively characterize the limited, we shall answer that in every case they appear as *positively* introducing a characterization of this type. An illusion? Granted. But what is the relation of this illusion to absolute knowledge? It is obviously

[4] We might add that, on the other hand, it cannot be of any value from the standpoint of the absolute; since from that standpoint (if this makes any sense at all) the finite is not.

an element which must be transformed and which by the
fact of the transformation is amplified, so to speak, so that
it becomes that knowledge itself. Transformation, we said;
that is, a passage from one to the other. It seems then that
the illusion has a nature, something positive (in a mysterious
sense) which makes it resistant, as such, to any transformation. We shall not challenge that the illusion has a truth
and that this truth is reducible to absolute knowledge ideally
posited. But it seems illegitimate to reduce *the fact of the
illusion* to the ideal truth which is its ground. The fact of
the illusion is reducible to an affirmation characterized by
the limitation it implies and which would cease being itself
if we transformed it by abstracting from this limitation itself.[5] We shall admit, then, without insisting here on the
philosophical consequences of this distinction, that we must
not, or that we cannot, assimilate the existence of error (or
of the finite) to its ideal content. It would seem then that we
are faced with this dilemma: (1) Either error, as existence,
is assimilated, as such, by absolute knowledge; *qua* error, it
is part of the nature of absolute knowledge. But then absolute knowledge ceases to be an intelligible system; if the finite

[5] It is not difficult to see the serious problem arising here: Is
thought entirely content? Can we reject the form of this content as
we would a negligible accident? But, in any case, accident does not
mean negation; from the fact that for certain logical ends we can
ignore the conditions accompanying thought and treat them like a
limitation, it does not follow that, when we adopt the standpoint of
absolute knowledge, we have the right to uphold this separation and
even, going further, to treat this limitation like an absolute negation.

exists in it as such, then it must include true elements and hence it is not absolute. (2) Or error, as existence, is excluded from absolute knowledge, which in this case assimilates only the truth of the finite; the absolute is only the concentration of this truth. But it is immediately clear that this solution is contradictory; absolute knowledge excludes a certain mode of positing ideas, which is, properly speaking, the finite; hence, that knowledge seems to cease being absolute. Perhaps we could present the contradiction in a more striking way. There is a distinction between the finite *in se* (whether or not it be pure negation)—that is, the finite considered in its abstract nakedness—and the finite reduced to an intelligible essence which is, itself, identical in the final analysis with absolute knowledge. There exists a distinction between two points of view, and this distinction is not encompassed within absolute knowledge; absolute knowledge expresses only one aspect, not the concrete totality of which the two aspects are only two abstract moments. Better: absolute knowledge, which should be the affirmation of the identity of the ideal and the real, is now posited as only and exclusively ideal. There remains a duality between the ideal and the real, a duality which absolute knowledge cannot encompass.

Let us take one more step: absolute knowledge (the ideal totality of essences) and the level of the finite can only present themselves as two elements of a higher totality which includes them in itself; but, either this totality is one with absolute knowledge, which then is both element and totality at the same time, which is contradictory, or, if this totality is greater than knowledge, it is unknowable in itself, it is a substance to which knowledge is reducible without anyone being able to understand how.[6] If we reject these two alternatives, we have no way out but an infinite regress; and absolute knowledge ought to transcend any regress of this type.

The second solution then appears as ruinous as the first. Let us review the preceding conclusions and try to determine their exact scope. It had seemed to us that the absolute had to be an infinite and concrete intelligible system, absolute knowledge. In the abstract it seemed that it could not exclude anything and at the same time had to be a perfect unity, the elements of which have only an incomplete, ideal existence. There were two requirements which could be formulated as follows:

(1) The imperfect must exist, *qua* imperfect, in the absolute itself; otherwise it is outside of it, and the absolute is nothing more than a content, an ideal construction.

(2) The imperfect cannot exist, *qua* imperfect, in the abso-

[6] We might be tempted to conceive absolute knowledge as a form of the substance of which the finite as such is the content. But the absurdity of this solution is clear; for in the substance form and content must be at least absolutely adequate to each other, if not identical. And what equivalence can there be between the finite and the infinite?

lute itself; otherwise the latter is nothing but a chain of elements which subsist as elements and do not constitute a true system.

These two equally essential requirements, then, turn out to be contradictory and cannot be met at one and the same time. Absolute knowledge cannot be both a total encompassment and an intelligible system; if we are permitted to use the expression, it cannot be at once extensively and intensively absolute, and, on the other hand, it is nothing at all if it is not both. It would seem that the affirmation of a perfect, intelligible system to which nothing would be exterior, and which would in its unity encompass the finite thought of the various minds as its abstract moments, turns out to be ambiguous and even illusory.

But if, giving up this idea of absolute knowledge, we try to find out what really positive note there is in it, what shall we find? No doubt, we must abandon the hope of reinstating the finite in the absolute and we must concede that the finite as such remains outside this absolute itself. But in what sense then can we affirm the unity of truth? We do not believe it is possible to deny that this unity is an absolute requirement of the mind. Our purpose here is not at all to oppose intellectualism, but to try to determine its limits and its exact scope. We find ourselves, it seems to me, before two conceptions that are both incomplete and irreconcilable, and the unity of which, if it were possible, would be absolute knowledge. Of these two conceptions, one, it seems, must be rejected as illusory; it is the one according to which the absolute is the result of a mere addition of the finite. It is immediately evident that this addition is inconceivable; furthermore, the absolute, as we have seen, can in no way be conceived as the product of a juxtaposition of elements; and the elements disappear from the point of view of the absolute, for the absolute is prior by right and by necessity. This addition would only be possible through the illegitimate extension of a method which is applicable only to the level of the finite. With regard to positing the absolute (intellectually conceived) as finite, we would have here a ruinous concession to which no reasoning mind could reconcile itself. There remains the second conception which we should like to formulate as follows: Can the absolute be conceived as a system which would englobe within itself the truth of the finite and only its truth, a system which would be something like an ideal concentration, something like a perfect view of what appears in the finite as irrationally scattered and is therefore only the finite imperfectly viewed? One might immediately observe that, in one sense, nothing lies outside of this system (because no truth can be posited outside of it) and that, in another sense, everything lies outside of it (since the imperfect modes of understanding are necessarily excluded from its essence). It seems to us that the affirmation of a system of this type is implied in every act of thought, for it is impossible to conceive what the notion of truth means if it is not reducible to the idea of such a system.

Before asking ourselves how we should interpret that notion of truth, we must first face certain objections which cannot help but be thrown up at us. First of all, this one: How can this system be infinite if the imperfect modes of understanding lie outside of it? There can be no doubt as to the answer. Indeed, in what sense does this externality exist? In the sense that there is no reduction possible from one to the other, that it is impossible to pass from a lower level of truth to the level of absolute truth. It is precisely in this way that the finite lies outside of the infinite; to the extent to which we make of the infinite a fixed thing, to which we turn it into a being whose limit would characterize it in a positive way, there is no doubt that we must consider the finite as being outside of the infinite. For, as such, *qua* finite, it cannot be absorbed by the infinite; but if we look at its essence (which in this case plays the role of the truth of the finite or, rather, is only a particular expression of it), this will no longer be true, and the externality will disappear. Thus there is truly a sense in which the finite and the infinite are external to each other, and a sense in which this externality disappears.

Another objection would be this: it seems possible that there should be an addition of the truth of the ideal system and of that which is scattered in the finite; consequently, the ideal system is not perfectly, supremely true. The answer is obvious: the objection would be valid against any sort of extensive conception of truth, not against a theory which would consider truth to be something perfectly interior, an absolutely comprehensive unity. But could we not be accused of embracing as our own the very notion of the finite which we had criticized and of utilizing the concept of negation in an illegitimate way? It is important, we believe, to make a distinction here; and the distinction that must be brought in corresponds in a certain sense to the one we made relative to externality. No doubt, if the finite were only a negation, the Hegelian or Neo-Hegelian conception would be valid; and this is what we have denied. But from the fact that it is more than a negation, it does not follow that it is in no way and in no sense a negation. The finite, we believe, is a negation which affirms, a negation which somehow imitates the positive and concrete affirmation of being. If we consider only the content, that is, if we adopt a rigorously intellectual point of view, we shall reduce the finite to a mere negation; but this way we shall end up with nothing but an abstract view from which no metaphysical conclusion can be drawn. In order to have a chance of getting somewhere, we must keep in mind the special manner of positing the negation which qualifies it and makes it exist, so to speak, with an existence that is illusory only by comparison. But it is nonetheless true that, if we limit ourselves to what we have called the intellectual point of view, it is legitimate to identify the finite with a negation; that really is, we repeat, only a provisional and vague way to think about all this.

In any case, we are going to be led now to delve into the very notion of the finite, because we have to ask ourselves in what sense a truth of the finite is possible.

But first it is important that we ask ourselves in what sense an absolute system is possible. A first conception might consist in considering it as an ideal of finite thought toward which the latter would move progressively. But it is immediately clear that the characteristic of this ideal would be that it could not be reached. Indeed, let us suppose this knowledge to be completed. If finite thought forms itself into a system which absorbs the world into itself, will the evolution of this thought in action have to be posited as governed by laws? If it is not subject to any laws, the knowledge ceases to be absolute; there is a sphere of contingency which remains beyond its reach. We must then admit that it is governed by a certain determinism. Is this determinism knowable by finite thought which we suppose to be completed? If it is not, this thought is not knowledge of an absolute kind; if it is, there will again arise the question of knowing whether the understanding of this determinism is itself governed by laws, and so on ad infinitum; this endless regress reveals an internal contradiction to which we must pay attention. Can we get around it by negating the dualism of the law and the understanding of the law? But, besides the fact that it is difficult to avoid the problem of the nature of virtual laws (which can only be solved, it seems, if we have recourse to a transcendent mind), would the situation improve if we posited the absolute autonomy of thought? Absolute knowledge would become relative to pure freedom, which would destroy it as absolute. Moreover, we might point out that the passage of finite thought to absolute knowledge (that is, to the negation of the limit) is impossible.

We come then to the conclusion that absolute knowledge as the ideal of finite thought cannot exist. But had not this absolute knowledge appeared to us as reality itself? Hence, must we not say that, from the point of view which we adopted, reality and existence appear as inevitably dissociated? We conclude, therefore, that for finite thought (at least *qua* knowledge) *reality can in no way be posited as existing.* This is in our eyes the deep and hidden meaning of the transcendental dialectic.

We must now go further into the problem itself of the nature of existence. Existence, we shall say, and this is only a provisional definition, means to be given to a consciousness in general.[7] Existence is linked to thought insofar as the latter is capable of receiving some datum, that is, insofar as it is finite. This amounts to saying that existence, to a

[7] With regard to this matter, we could insist on the difference there is between this definition, which is a critical definition, and the definition given of existence by empirical Idealism.

degree which must be further defined, is a limit; it is, more exactly, the limit-function exercised with regard to finite thought by the datum relative to this thought. It seems more exact to define existence as a function than as an act of positing, as Kant would have it (Kant may have been at fault in not clarifying his thought which, on this point, may have lent itself to realist interpretations that were not too well founded). Perhaps it might be better to say that existence is a moment, an ideal moment, linked to the essence[8] of finite thought. Thought, as such, seems clearly to be liberated from existence, which it conditions. There is more: existence, which is relative to thought, is also intrinsically relative. The reason for this is that a limit cannot really be external to thought; thought can only become aware of its limits by transcending them; and this amounts to saying that these limits are posited as contingent in relation to thought, and that up to a certain point it negates them. Where there is a limit, there is progress, since there is a demand for greater depth. Existence resolves itself into becoming (a succession of limtis that are negated while they are posited); if this becoming is considered as content, as an outline of an intelligible system, it is preferable to call it essence. To say that the essence (a particular essence) exists is the same as saying that it has presented itself to thought

[8] It is important here not to take the word essence in its exact meaning. Is the finiteness of thought anything else but a deficiency of the essence? This problem will be examined later.

under this successive and limited form, that finite thought in general can only grasp it in this form.

Thus we see clearly that the point of view of existence is relative. Does this point of view exist for an absolute mind? We have seen that, even for finite thought, every limit is contingent and remains internal to it. These limits are nonetheless real in the sense that they are the necessary conditions of the development by which finite thought becomes conscious of itself; they are, if we can use the expression, essentially ideal and accidentally real. Is absolute thought subject, and can it be conceived as subject, to an internal development? Such is the meaning of the problem we have put forth. But since an immanent development necessarily implies some kind of finality, this comes down to asking if it is possible to conceive of finality as governing absolute thought. It would seem that the answer to this question is negative; for since the transcendence of this finality in relation to the datum which it governs seems to be established,[9] it would seem necessary to admit a form of finality that is above absolute thought; and this would lead us into a contradictory realism. Thus, it seems certain that the moment we posit absolute thought, we must give up trying to find in it an immanent development.

If, then—and this is the last possible hypothesis—we af-

---

[9] By this we mean that finality cannot be explained from the standpoint of the elements, and that we are obliged to conceive these insights as abstract finite views of an indivisible whole.

firm the transcendence of absolute thought with regard to any finite thought, we must resign ourselves to fixing and concentrating this absolute thought beyond the temporal order. Yet an ambiguity remains: atemporal can mean basically independent with regard to time, that the idea of time cannot be applied to a certain reality (it is in this sense that mathematical truths are atemporal); atemporal can also mean the limit-concentration of a duration (it is impossible to abstract from duration, but we reduce it to being only an indivisible unit). In what sense can we posit absolute thought as atemporal? It seems, if it is in the first sense, that we strip it of all consciousness. How, indeed, can we affirm that duration is not reducible to the act of consciousness? Or rather, is not the latter the maximum of concentration of the former in the sense that it would contain all duration in potency? But absolute thought, negated both as ideal and as consciousness, is nothing but a substance which Idealism could not exploit. If it is not the ideal of a consciousness, it has to be an actual consciousness. Consequently, it includes within itself a relation (vanishing) to duration. Let us examine this hypothesis and ask ourselves whether it is acceptable. Does the hypothesis of an absolute consciousness satisfy the demands which brought about its invention? We began with the fact that every act of knowledge presupposes completed knowledge. From our present standpoint, and if the hypothesis is true, this formula should lend itself to the following transposition: the act of a finite consciousness, we shall say, implies the positing of an absolute consciousness; we might conclude from this that the development of finite consciousnesses is the unfolded imitation of absolute consciousness; and thus finite consciousness produces truth by reproducing within itself the content of absolute consciousness. But it is easy to see that either this conception is reducible to an unacceptable and meaningless realism or it implies an intelligible link between finite consciousness and absolute consciousness. This link then is thought itself, and we are back to the conceptions which we criticized previously. Truth cannot become hypostatized in a consciousness; in relation to Idealism, spiritualism is not a step forward, but rather the contrary; and, on the other hand, Idealism is forced to posit an absolute knowledge which falls apart while being affirmed.

What conclusions can be drawn from this ensemble of critical remarks? Upon what do the multiple contradictions which we have pointed out rest? Upon this, that we have hypostatized a requirement of thought and that we have thought it possible to isolate and consider by itself the pseudo-reality thus obtained. The philosophers of absolute knowledge are the victims, it seems, of the same illusion as the naïve realists. They think it possible to break the link uniting the object (here, absolute knowledge) with the subject and to treat the object like a being, without taking notice that this being owes its reality to its participation in the subject. Absolute knowledge, like matter or life, is still only another abstraction, even, as it is true, if it is the highest and most concrete. Let us for an instant suppose to be constituted and completed the dialectic which would make of the real a perfectly intelligible system, establishing, so to speak, an intelligible traffic among notions; still, this dialectic, this system, would only be a series of products relative to the act by which they had been posited, and whatever concreteness they had they would draw from the act of concrete affirmation which would have established them. Absolute knowledge then seems to be inevitably ideal, and that only inevitably relative to a pure subjectivity, from which it can detach itself only by an illegitimate abstraction. Does this lead us back to a fearful critical philosophy which would hold as the only reality the act of consciousness where the subject and object are unified? It does not seem so. For this act germinally contains all the contradictions which we have pointed out; it tends toward absolute knowledge as its fulfillment; and we have seen that it cannot reach that mark. But, one might insist, in spite of everything does not this reality have to be at least immanent in the act of consciousness? A number of ambiguities must be cleared up. In the sense that absolute knowledge is *immanent* in the act of consciousness, the word cannot apply to reality since the latter does not and cannot coincide with absolute knowledge. It seems that it cannot be a question of that "intellectual immanence" which is reducible, in the last analysis, to an implication of notions. Even supposing that dialectical development like that of the *Doc-*

trine of Science is possible starting with the Cogito, this development could only be conceived as completed by an arbitrary act of the mind which would reveal its abstract and ideal character. In other words, to say it once more, the relation of the Cogito to absolute knowledge, a relation outside of which no intellectualist metaphysics can be formed, is a false relation upon which only a science devoid of any real claims, of any ontological requirements, can be based. In the system which a metaphysics of this type tends to erect, there is no room for being, as Schelling saw so well. Does it follow from this that being is in no way and in no sense immanent in the act of consciousness? It suffices to reflect a moment upon what a negation of this type would imply in order to understand its absurdity. To deny purely and simply all immanence of being in consciousness is to deny the relation of thought to the real; it is consequently either to deny absolutely that there is any reality, or, like the realists, while positing the real, to exclude it from thought, that is, to negate it. The contradictions of realism have been too well exposed by the history of philosophy; it is useless for us to go over them again. Is the first solution any more acceptable? Clearly, it is not; the negation of reality presupposes a certain conception of the real (in general, Eleatic); and, if we get right down to it, to negate absolutely the real amounts, for thought, to giving up thinking itself either by an irrational act of desperation or in view of rational ends which thought, if it is logical, must precisely identify with the real. Moreover, whatever we might think of this last hypothesis, it appears clear that, once realism is rejected, once the ghost of substantialism has vanished, the synthetic identification of being and thoughts is at least unassailable, provided, however, this identification does not lead to the notion of absolute knowledge and is not inextricably linked to it (to say the truth, it necessarily leads to it). The only thing that remains then, we repeat, is that the negation of the real is a kind of unjustified suicide, of a leap into the unknown, something to which thought can in no way be condemned. If neither of the two alternatives just presented is acceptable, immanence must somehow be affirmed. Before asking ourselves in what sense it can be legitimately affirmed, let us try to discover through what necessity thought is constrained to posit it (in whatever manner it might be). It is evident from what has already been said that, for thought, to negate being absolutely or to posit it outside of itself unconditionally amounts to the same thing: as a matter of fact, Idealism developed, above all, from the moment when this basic identity of realism and acosmism[10] was understood. The transcendental esthetic, if we abstract from the thing in itself, is certainly dominated by the awareness of this identity. Thus, if thought is outside of being, then it is only a form and finds in itself nothing substantial. To say that it is a form amounts to saying that it posits itself

[10] Acosmism is used here in a sense that is slightly different from the usual sense, but there seems to be no word to designate a philosophy that would negate reality.

as a form, since the determinations of reflexive thought are never different from those which thought posits in itself. This substantiality which it lacks is again something posited (*gesetzt*), not something discovered (*gefunden*); it is true that it immediately becomes something ideal and, precisely, being, from the point of view where we place ourselves, is nothing more than a purely ideal correlative which floats in front of the mind (*vorschwebt*) and which the latter, by its own means, at each moment converts into thought. But, according to the initial postulate, there is in this process nothing but the accidental, nothing which is really being. And yet it is clear that, between such a philosophy and an Idealism like that of Fichte which posits the identity of being and thought, the difference is only one of intention (*Meinung*), to use the Hegelian expression. In other words, absolutely excluding being from thought and affirming their identity are basically identical acts. We already know for what reason this identity cannot be accepted. But then in what sense can we speak of immanence? We know now that there is a relation between being and thought and that, on the other hand, this relation is not that of pure and simple identity. How must this relation be understood? Given a thinking mind, for example, a state of consciousness, in what sense is there being in this thought, in this state of consciousness? If we exclude a realism that owes its apparent meaningfulness to the metaphors with which it covers itself, what answer comes to mind? If the identity is accepted as a postulate, the being of the thought under consideration is reduced to being nothing else but what in it is really *thought*, namely, what in it can be assimilated to reflection, that is, to the intelligible; we know how the passage takes place, one thing leading to another, from this nucleus to the total system and how the nucleus becomes real only in relation to the system which, itself, is nothing else but the totality of true thought. On the other hand, we have seen why this way of interpreting knowledge is unacceptable and contradictory. How can it be improved? It is evident that, as long as we adopt the standpoint of truth, the standpoint of essence, this interpretation is the only one possible. But the moment we have discovered the essential relativity of this standpoint, things are different. Here a remark must immediately be made: that it is impossible to go back from any single element of knowledge to the real. Since this element implies, if it is to cease being abstract, the totality (unthinkable anyway) of knowledge, nowhere within that knowledge can the question of the real arise; nor does this question even arise when the totality of knowledge is hypostatized since this totality is itself ideal and it is impossible to convert it into reality. But then how is this problem to be presented? Excluding it is impossible, as we have seen, since, on the one hand, thought implies something real and, on the other, it is not identical with this reality; there is participation of thought in reality. How is this participation to be understood? The only road open to us seems to be the following:

to examine the act of knowledge itself (*qua* relation) and
see how from this act (*Tätigkeit überhaupt*) a passage to
reality is possible. A priori it seems certain that we shall find
here in a seminal state, so to speak, all the difficulties, all the
contradictions, which make the idea of absolute knowledge
unthinkable. In other words, we doubt that these difficulties
and contradictions stem from the actualization of the unconditioned, as Hamilton and, to a certain extent, Kant
himself believed. This actualization is already implied, ultimately, in the elementary act of knowledge itself, since every
act, insofar as it is an object, tends to find its completion in
a system.

But then what is this contradiction which vitiates the
act of knowledge itself, and which strips it of all metaphysical value? It seems to reside very simply in the fact that all
knowledge implies an "unknowable" as its necessary condition. Let there be no misunderstanding: this is not the
unknowable of agnosticism, which is still an object and the
concept of which disintegrates as soon as it is posited, since it
is nothing but knowledge beyond knowledge. When Spencer
says that the essential nature of energy or of matter is unknown to us, he means that the true properties of energy or
of matter necessarily lie beyond our minds, the latter being
conceived by Spencer, here in agreement with Hamilton and
Mansell, only as a power to make things relative. But these
properties, after all, are determinations; as such, they are
still, in the most general and strongest sense, something

knowable; and if this knowable something is beyond us, it can only be for reasons that are contingent and imply no metaphysical necessity.[11] The same is true of Kantianism to the extent to which the theory of the thing-in-itself is interpreted in the usual fashion. Either there is no link, no passage, between our representations and the transcendental object, and the latter then in no way deserves the name of object—in the strongest sense we can say that it is not; or there *is* such a link and then this object fits into the finished system of knowledge. Thus it is evident that it is not in this sense that we can speak rationally of an "unknowable." That is unknowable, in the only legitimate sense of the word, which by definition lies beyond all knowledge, that is, which is a condition of knowledge. Now Kantianism has victoriously proven that the conditions of knowledge can only be subjective. Thus the level of subjectivity is that of the unknowable since it encompasses the condition of all possible knowledge.

According to what has just been said, the contradiction inherent in every act of knowledge would seem to lie, then, in the fact that knowledge always posits its object as real and that yet, in virtue of the fact that it is an object of knowledge, the object is only an abstraction. Absolute knowledge (the efforts to construct absolute knowledge) is pre-

[11] It goes without saying that Spencer's error is even more complete; he hypostatizes into objects what can only be categories of reflexive thought.

cisely the effort to go from the abstract to the concrete, to develop the entire content of the abstract; but this effort is fruitless (metaphysically); the flaw is too deep for such a remedy to be efficacious. This is because of the doubly abstract character (we can say both subjectively and objectively) of the object of knowledge, and it is because the object remains subjectively abstract that it is impossible to expand it into an objectively concrete totality; this totality itself remains an abstraction that is incapable of being constituted into being. The inability of the unconditioned to be actualized then stems from the intrinsic nature and character of any act of knowledge, as we mentioned earlier.

An important remark must be made here on the character of the unknowable thus defined. It would seem, first of all, that the unknowable as pure subject is only an abstraction, a form about which nothing can be said because it is empty. But, precisely, the pure subject appears abstract only from the moment when it is, as it were, posited as an object before itself. It is this conversion alone that makes it an abstraction, and the fact that we cannot predicate any determination of it insofar as it is posited as object proves precisely that this positing is not legitimate. Hence, we could say that in the pure subject there is a possibility of movement, but this movement is a fruitless self-repetition while the movement arising from the object, even if it cannot reach completion in a metaphysical totality, is at least a progressive enrichment, a tendency toward the concrete. In one case, therefore, the process is willed, so to speak, by the very nature of the object; in the other case, it cannot be pushed forward without violence being done to the *subject*. The duplication of the subect which puts it face to face with itself as object is an artificial operation, an operation without any real bearing. Far, then, from saying that the subject is a pure abstraction, it must be understood that it cannot be called an abstraction and that it is in itself the living source of the concrete. We may rightly ask ourselves at this point if we have not found the root of the idea of finite thought; perhaps the phenomenon that is finite thought has its source in this artificial duplication of the subject which posits it as an object while opposing it to the true object. Conceived in this manner, the notion of finite thought corresponds only to a provisional measure of the mind. But perhaps this notion itself is somehow only an image, a reflection, of another notion which on its part has metaphysical value. Absolute knowledge, we have seen, remains immanent in thought in the sense that, even if we suppose it to be completed, it continues to be suspended in the act that posits it; it is impossible to doubt that this act is thought itself. But then thought somehow limits knowledge on the side of the real. Thus thought is limiting rather than limited. But, someone might say, Is this not only a play on words? If knowledge remains outside of it, is not thought, in a certain sense at least, finite? This objection corresponds to a real difficulty (or perhaps to a series of difficulties); because of the ambiguity inherent in the act of knowledge which relates incompatible elements, it seems that the relation of knowledge to thought cannot be characterized in a determinate way. Consequently, insofar as there is nothing in common, we can well speak of reciprocal externality; but this immediately becomes inverted, for externality presupposes a common datum (for example, space); and it is necessary, therefore, if we talk about externality, that we admit the existence of a common principle to which thought and knowledge might both be external. We would be led then to posit something which would be the reality of knowledge and of thought. But let us not forget that between thought and knowledge there is not merely a simple correlation or opposition; knowledge exists for thought and through it. Knowledge and thought cannot then participate in being to the same degree and on the same basis. On the other hand, we must beware of one danger. It would not be right, according to what we have seen, to posit a direct participation of thought in being, thus considering knowledge as a kind of shadow or projection of thought itself. We have already seen that this projection is unthinkable and that it is not possible a priori to admit that knowledge is deduced from the Cogito. This impossibility should now appear clearer still. If thought as a condition of knowledge is absolutely unknowable, it is quite impossible that knowledge as a totality could be drawn from it by means of a development; for if this development were possible, thought would be nothing more than concentrated knowledge and the difficulty which we have discovered would reappear at the very heart of thought. There is no doubt that we have touched upon the principal difference between us and Fichte. Participation in being cannot then be conceived in such simple terms; we have to delve deeper, beyond knowledge, in order to discover a means of positing it.

It seems, in any case, that we already have a few important clues, at least negative ones, on the nature of this participation. We have seen, on the one hand, that it is impossible not to posit it (in a general way); on the other, that there is no communication between absolute knowledge and being; it is not as knowledge that thought can be said to participate in being.[12] Shall we find greater satisfaction in positing that thought participates in being insofar as it is a pure (unknowable) subject? The negation of the first thesis seems to send us back to the affirmation of the second. And yet, we are going to meet with a serious difficulty. For what does this second thesis amount to if not to this: thought posits its participation in being insofar as it is itself a pure subject. But what does this amount to? To the fact that thought tries to make an object of itself as pure subject and look at it as something out there in front of itself, thus trans-

[12] It may not be useless with regard to this expression, "thought *qua* knowledge," to point out that the dualism of what we have called thought and of knowledge is itself interior to pure thought in a more general sense. There is knowledge only through thought and for it; knowledge is thought considered under one of its aspects.

forming the unknowable into an object and consequently
into an abstraction? In these circumstances, does the affirmation have any meaning? The reasons why it seemed that the
pure subject (thought *qua* pure subject) must participate in
being lose their value as soon as the subject is transformed
into an object, fixed into a sterile abstraction. Hence, the
moment the participation in being of thought as pure subject
is *posited*, it ceases being thinkable (because the pure subject is turned into an object). It seems that two different
and opposed conclusions can be drawn from this: either the
contradiction lies in the *fact of positing (Setzung in sich
selbst)* participation in this fashion, or in positing it we make
explicit the contradiction inherent in the notion itself of
participation (thus conceived). We must pause before this
alternative and try to grasp its full meaning; for here we have
reached the outer limits of Idealism, where we can perhaps
pass over to a doctrine of being. Is there a contradiction in
the notion of the pure subject's participation in being? It is
important to understand that a priori this question is insoluble, for it can only be resolved (one way or the other)
through this notion being posited (by reflection), that is, by
converting the subject into an object; and this alters the
terms of the problem, or, rather, in order for a problem to
exist, this positing and conversion have to take place. What
are the results? We know that they are contradictory; but
it does not seem possible to find the cause of this contradiction since the elimination of one of the possible causes is *a*

priori excluded. It would seem that the only thing we can say is this: the contradiction only arises through the act of positing participation (whether it produces it or limits itself to making it explicit); it is only by a later act of reflection (hypothetical anyway) that it is possible to say that the contradiction is inherent in the notion itself. (Note moreover how improper the word notion is here: a notion implies a positing by reflection, while we should really be talking about an act prior to reflection.) Only by reflection is the contradiction at the heart of this act discovered. But let us even suppose that the hypothesis is *true* (that is, that it is inherent in the act itself); the word "true" suffices by itself to reveal the necessary intervention of reflection. Contradictions exist (admitting always that the first hypothesis is true, for in the other case this fact is immediately clear) only for reflection. Now, is what we have called the second act (hypothetical), which places the contradiction in the initial act of participation, legitimate? This displacement is only legitimate if in fact reflection has no other function but to make explicit the content of the act of participation. But, precisely, it seems that this interpretation, if our previous deductions are exact, is unacceptable (because in the end through the medium of reflection it would establish between the pure subject and knowledge a relation that could be translated into deductive language). More simply, the act of participation is apt to be seen as contradictory only if it is, to some extent, an act of intellection, containing within itself the seeds of later acts of reflection. But in whatever manner the act of participation must be conceived (granting the impossible, that it can properly speaking be conceived), it cannot be thought of in an intellectual fashion (under pain of becoming an element of knowledge), with the result that we cannot consider it contradictory in itself. It is not true to say, on the other hand, that it is merely an abstraction since every abstraction presupposes an act of reflection (which operates on an act of knowledge). Here again we can only speak of an abstraction by abstraction.[13]

The participation of thought (as pure subject) in being then is an act that reflection cannot posit (convert into a notion) without making it contradictory, the contradiction necessarily stemming from the fact that there is an incompatibility (logical discontinuity) between the act of participation and the act of reflection. Thus thought is led to affirm the impossibility of positing participation; but by this exclusion, it does not simply eliminate participation.[14] Ths case is not the same as that of a notion which thought cannot posit because it is contradictory (*qua* essence, e.g., a square circle); the contradiction lies, once again, not in the notion, but in

[13] One remark might present itself here to the reader's mind. Could it not be that the contradiction inherent in the fact of positing participation is the very contradiction which we have detected at the heart of every act of knowledge? We shall have occasion later on to examine, in order to reject or confirm it, this attractive (to say the least) hypothesis that would allow us to see clearly the relation that exists between knowledge and true participation.

[14] We have seen moreover how being is involved in thought itself.

the fact of converting participation into a notion. Participation at this point seems to be the upper limit of reflection, that is, the act before which all reflection must cease. As we know, there is no passage from participation to reflection.

Before going further, it might be useful to face a possible objection. The following could be said: it has been demonstrated that the relation constitutive of knowledge is one which is intrinsically devoid of reality (of being); hence, do we not have to conclude that its two terms are valid only in connection with their relation itself (as members of the relation) and, consequently, are equally devoid of metaphysical significance? Also it is difficult to see how the pure subject can be privileged with regard to the object (knowledge); in short: How it can participate in being?

The objection is strong and, it seems, can but be answered as follows: knowledge can only be posited as a relation for thought (synthetic); hence, the "subjective" term of this relation is not the pure subject, but the pure subject already converted into an object. Now, we have seen that the latter is an abstraction devoid of metaphysical value; nor is it that subject which participates in being. In short, the pure subject, apparently, cannot be considered as a term of the relation of knowing unless it is negated as subject, unless it is converted into an object. Hence, knowledge does not present itself as a contradiction, but only as the determination of an unknown in terms of an unknowable; it is the relation posited by an unknowable between itself (converted into an object) and the object which ultimately is identical with absolute knowledge. Here another obscure point arises: for as soon as thought posits knowledge, the internal progress of the latter becomes unintelligible to the former,[15] and thought must call upon itself (as unknowable) to account for it. To posit knowledge, to make a relation out of it, is to immobilize it and to condemn oneself, in order to explain that knowledge, to introducing into it a principle which transcends it. It seems, then, that the hypothesis proposed above on the identity of the two contradictions is verified, and that it is right to consider knowledge as posited participation, that is, negated as such. Perhaps we shall return to this very important point later on.

There are still other difficulties to face. We might be tempted to ask whether this participation is not identical with the most immediate knowledge, which is also a limit of reflection. Here the answer is very simple: for while this immediate knowledge only becomes clear by the light of reflection and relies on reflection (with regard to concepts), participation, as we know, excludes any relation to reflection. Thus it seems that reflexive activity operates between two limits, of which one is entirely ideal (absolutely immediate knowledge) and the other is participation in being. Neither the one nor the other can be *posited*; but this impossibility is based on opposite reasons in both cases. Absolutely immediate knowledge is complete indetermination; it

[15] An abstraction cannot account for it.

is, if you will, existence in general (setting aside the essence), and it corresponds to the matter of Neoplatonism (translated into the language of critical philosophy).

But then an even more serious difficulty arises: we are led to admit, in opposition to the principles of Idealism, a fundamental dichotomy between being and the idea of being. Here then is the ultimate objection, a singularly serious one, too. We have attempted to establish that thought cannot negate being; and it is from the necessity of positing being (in some definite relation to thought) that we have reached, by means of a sinuous argument, the theory just expounded. But when we come right down to it, could this first demonstration really bear on being and not just on the idea of being? We did not have to make this distinction as long as we remained within the fold of Idealism, but now it comes up again and we cannot disregard it. If our demonstration has resulted in establishing that the idea of being is a necessity of thought, there is a discontinuity in the theory as a whole since we have been led to speak of being in itself. So once again we must ask the question: Why is the negation of being impossible for thought? We have seen that the only way for thought to negate being is to identify itself with it. Is this manner of solving the problem acceptable and definitive? In other words, is this identification possible? Under what conditions would it be, and are these conditions realized? First, we can say that, in order for thought to identify itself with being, it must distinguish the latter from itself by an initial act, or again, posit within itself a relation between itself (as objectivized subject) and being. This relation is obviously the very relation of knowledge; being then is absolute knowledge. But we have seen why thought cannot be identified with absolute knowledge and why, after that identification, something is left over on the side of thought. To summarize, thought can only negate being by identifying itself with it (otherwise it posits it as completely external, which is unthinkable, or it posits it as having a relation of participation with it); and, on the other hand, this identification is impossible. We see then why the confusion which we feared does not exist; for it would only be possible to say that we are talking about the idea of being in the event of such an identification, that is, if thought negated being (as being). But the demonstration results directly in setting aside this interpretation.

Participation can only be an object of thought to the extent to which thought can strip itself of every element of reflection, to which it can renounce itself, set itself aside, so to speak; and this original act, by which it abdicates, is what from here on we shall call faith. It is to be noted that faith bears neither on being nor even on participation in general (since the scope of the demonstration extends up to that point) but on the participation of the object, as unknowable, in being. To the extent to which there is an (inverse) symmetry between the relation of the pure subject and being, on one side, and that of objective thought and existence, on the other, we can say that faith bears on the existence of God. But it is clear that this expression must not be taken literally. God does not exist; He is infinitely above existence since He is beyond all truth and can only be grasped by faith through the act which links Him intimately to thought. Can we now delve further into the nature of this participation? It seems to be essentially a mystery, that is, it eludes any analytic method that would convert it into an object.

But one more objection remains to be examined. We said earlier that the analysis of the act of knowledge leads to thought as a pure unknowable subject. But how can this pure subject be posited without being converted into an abstraction? Or rather, since the position necessarily involves this conversion, how can thought avoid being taken in by this abstraction? The question is very important since it seems that we have to choose between these two alternatives: (a) thought can, without contradiction, conceive itself as unknowable, but then it can also conceive itself as participating in being; (b) thought cannot, without contradiction, conceive itself as participation in being, but then it cannot even legitimately conceive itself as unknowable. Either the contradiction does not exist at all—or its scope is greater than it seemed at first. The problem, then, is to discover how thought can posit itself as unknowable.

Thought, we have said, takes the act of knowledge as its object. But let us not be deceived by words; it is only metaphorically that the act of knowledge can be likened to a true object. Thought immediately recognizes itself as present in this act, and it is precisely this recognition, the possibility of which is difficult to grasp; Thought distinguishes in the act an objective element and a subjective element, but the analysis shows the latter to be nothing but an abstraction; it seems that a new and original act is needed by which thought would become aware of the act of abstraction that distorts it in its own eyes, of the necessity in virtue of which *thought* posits *itself* before *itself* as *other*. Thought cannot compare itself as thinking with itself as *thought* (a term in the relation of knowledge); for it would be *qua* thinking that it would be setting up this comparison, and the comparison would be abolishing the first of its terms. Thus it is clear why no logical passage from the subject of knowledge to pure thought (which sets up the relation) is possible and why any such passage would result in a fruitless infinite regress. Through an act of transcendence which is above all reflection and is immediate in the sense that it transcends all mediation, thought affirms its identity with the subject; this act is an intellectual intuition that we shall define as follows: intellectual intuition is the act by which thought (as pure subject) affirms its identity with the subject of the relation of knowledge posited as an object. Thought thus raises the subject of knowledge up to its own level and affirms that its own complete freedom resides in that subject. Clearly, the intellectual intuition is the preliminary condition of faith and inaugurates a new type of intelligibility.

III

Notes, 1912-1913

[*Manuscript XIV*]

A. *Notes on the Ground of Values*

We have seen[16] that if we posit a psychological foundation to values, either we limit ourselves to bypass the metaphysical problems or we are led to give it an unacceptable solution, that is, to define values in terms of needs, of conditions of fact, and to think of being as something above values (as something indeterminate) unless it is as an intelligible system; and this leads to difficulties that are no doubt inextricable.

We cannot then avoid positing a metaphysical foundation to values, that is, to use traditional language, conceiving a relation between the good and being. This relation cannot be an objective identification (except perhaps ultimately, and then at that level it loses all real significance), since being, when posited objectively, cannot be anything but a sys-

[16] This is a reference to a text that has not yet been identified. (Editor's note.)

tem of essences and negates itself as metaphysics. Being then
is not the good; we know that an objective affirmation on
being can have no metaphysical import. The good cannot be
conceived in terms of being, but only in terms of participation. Before proceeding further, perhaps it is necessary to
recall what is the precise meaning of the idea of participation.

There is being only for me; this is true, not in the superficial and neocritical sense that refuses to posit a *representa-
tum* outside its relation to what is represented, but in the
entirely different sense that the affirmation of being only has
value insofar as it is not the position or idea of an object but,
rather, true participation, a creation. For the fruitless identity of being that is, must be substituted the fruitful act by
which *I am* (the synthesis of the ego and being). In this
sense participation is defined as a concrete life, the isolated
elements of which are nothing but lifeless abstractions, objects. Being, therefore, is neither substance nor representation. It can only be conceived as that in which thought participates.

What is clear is that wherever there is creativity, that is to
say, affirmation, to some degree there is participation. But
obviously various difficulties arise here. First of all, is there
some degree of participation wherever there is thought? We
already know that this question cannot be formulated this
way; and this, because participation cannot be conceived as
the real content of thought (in the sense in which the Neo-

Hegelians say that every judgment bears on reality). There is participation only where there is thought about participation, but this thought can dominate the lower levels of thought enough to confer new dignity upon them.

From this we conclude that the love of one creature for another is not *in itself* the love of God, but only that the mind which has elevated itself to participation finds that same participation in the acts in which God does not seem to be present. Faith possesses a power of expansion which translates itself into interpretation; this interpretation is not fictitious because it is beyond the level where the distinction between the fictitious and the true still has meaning. Here we stumble on the seemingly very strong objection that the interpretations do not agree and therefore are nothing but fairy tales. That these interpretations do not converge is something which can be affirmed a priori, for such a convergence would be the sign of an ideal content which cannot but be defective.[17] As to calling them fairy tales, this is to bring back into the religious domain the fundamentally extra-religious idea of a nature (of some truth). Religion as seen from the outside cannot help giving the appearance of being the level of the absolutely arbitrary. It seems that we are led thereby to pure nihilism—unless we can discover some harmony, some order, in which the various revelations (the creative interpretations) would naturally become inte-

[17] In this sense and for this reason one could not use these contradictions among religious attitudes in arguing against religion.

grated. On the other hand, this harmony would risk being conceived as some kind of truth, an objective content; and then everything would crumble. There would be a true integration only if this harmony were itself a creative interpretation, a faith, and not the affirmation of an objective order of these revelations.

Are we led then to posit an uncoordinated multiplicity of religious attitudes? Does the theory of participation lead us only into chaos?

But this plurality of distinct objects is only possible in the world of knowledge; and, on the other hand, knowledge cannot be satisfied with this uncoordinated plurality. This idea of a multiplicity of experiences lies between metaphysics and the science of religions which tries to determine the relationships between them.

Must metaphysics then be considered a transcendent exhortation? A logic of freedom which can only determine from the outside what the conditions are under which participation is conceivable? Only, here again it seems that a disastrous dilemma awaits us: either this parenesis will depend on contingent psychological data—or it will lead to religious formalism. The first alternative is no doubt immediately set aside. But what about the second? It is evident that in religious matters the dualism of matter and form is impossible; this dualism is only the abstract schema of the level of truths. However, are we not trapped with our backs to this schema? It seems that there might be conditions that are essential to all participation and into which particular and contingent contexts (matters) could be subsumed. But we must not forget that participation necessarily includes the affirmation of the noncontingency of this context.[17a] But there is no "truth" of this affirmation. The essential act of religion is the negation of the dualism of matter and form, and there is no valid metaphysical critique of this act. But then are we not faced once again with the intellectually discouraging idea of an indefinite plurality of affirmations? We will repeat that these affirmations, thus posited, become ideas. There is no possible metaphysical utilization of the study of religions; such study can only be a weapon against religion and, on the other hand, no valid argument can be based on it. There is religion only if we close our eyes to everything which presents itself empirically as religion.

We must limit ourselves, then, to the idea that metaphysics, in the last analysis, is a transcendent exhortation based on a critique.

But we are not yet free from difficulties. Will this metaphysics have only a maieutic function, its role consisting in facilitating individual religious creations? This is not the pragmatic role, so to speak, that it is fitting to give it; its true

[17a] Marcel means that it is not accidentally that the particular events of my life take place the way they do. A meeting with a particular person, for example, is part and parcel of the very fabric of my life and of its significance. In a theistic context, we could say that in the eyes of God everything that happens to me is or can be an occasion of grace or growth.

function consists in restoring to us the meaning, the notion
of the individual. This metaphysics makes us understand
and re-create while understanding. From this standpoint,
what is the relation between metaphysics and its object?
Does it generate the latter or reproduce it by a kind of ideal
generation? In short, can metaphysics be conceived as a destruction?[18] It is evident that it cannot; for if this were the
case, metaphysics could succeed either in dogmatically de-
stroying religion (which would become an ideal content) or
would determine the categories of religious thought, and this
would reinstate the dualism of matter and form. The same is
true if metaphysics is conceived as a critique. Looking at this
matter more closely, let us ask ourselves if it is not superficial
to try to force metaphysics into a framework that does not
befit it. We have seen that we are led to posit the noncontingency of the empirical relationship (a relationship that links
individual thought to a given experience), that is, to affirm
that the distinction itself between matter and form loses all
validity on the religious level. But then either of two things
is true: either this act, itself, is a form and presupposes the
dualism that it negates—or we have, at the very outset, gone
beyond this dualism and we operate on another level. Can
we say that the thought which is embodied in this act is a
form? Let us recall how our dialectical reasoning defines this
act, and how it is led to it: this reasoning consists in noting
that the contingency of the empirical relationship cannot be

[18] Doubtful reading. (Editor's note.)

conceived as truth and that, on the other hand, there can be no "truth" of this relationship. Positing this relationship as contingent is possible only for a free mind which fetters itself and negates itself; the free mind which strives to realize itself, to actualize itself, cannot but affirm the noncontingency of this relationship (refuse to posit individuality as thought in general). It is in this sense that dialectical reasoning could be defined as a logic of freedom. But by conceiving it in this way, do we not establish it as a formal ordering? Is not the dialectic an ordered succession of acts by thought in general? The answer must be that the dialectic is an ensemble of acts by which thought in general becomes individual. At the top of the dialectic, there is the determined, but the determined fecundated by the level of pure thought. The dialectic is nothing but the movement of a thinking mind which withdraws more and more from what is purely formal and grasps its contradictions more and more clearly. The dialectic addresses a mind in general only insofar as this mind in general contains an individuality that it strives to actualize. It is the call of one free mind to other free minds. It is a living word addressed to living beings (and not the reader *in se*, a thought schema for which there are apodictic and impersonal certainties). It opens the doors to the world of living thought. The dialectic can exist only if it ends in life and personal certainties. It teaches the way to personal life and personal certitude.

The key to the whole theory of participation is, it must be

repeated, the act by which thought discovers that it would
be negating its freedom by positing the dualism of matter
and form; the practical principle of individuality is found,
then, in the negation of the contingency of the relationship
to experience, in acceptance. But this acceptance is not a
stoical adherence to the eternal order of which I am only one
element (this adherence is still only the practical negation of
freedom). It is not an adherence; it is an act of willing, of
willing oneself—this is the essence of the act we are dealing
with—but not willing oneself such as we are, subordinating
one's will to a given nature. The acceptance, therefore, is
only the basis of a desire for conversion.[19] This desire is not,
as we know, the form of a will in general; it betrays itself as
soon as it ceases being love and faith, that is to say, participation. Grace is nothing but the distance between this desire
of participation and psychological individuality; it is this
desire itself represented in terms of being, grasped objectively
and constructed as an external cause. Grace is a true notion
in the completely negative sense that there is not and cannot

[19] It seems that the practical acceptance of an empirical reality
conceived as noncontingent is symbolized best in the act positing this
reality as willed by God. From this standpoint, we can better understand the deep meaning of the solution to the problem of the relations between freedom and grace; this problem is insoluble only for
those who objectivize the act of positing the noncontingency of the
empirical relationship into an exterior being to whom is attributed a
causality that is somehow physical (while this causality is and must
be only a symbolization of the creative act by which thought affirms
its freedom by negating the dualism of matter and form).

be any "truth" of an affirmation that would make this act of the will, this freedom, depend upon an ensemble of given or actualized tendencies. The dualism of nature and grace cannot be transcended: this is the price of freedom.

It is clear in what sense we are led both to justify and to go beyond monadism. Monadism is true insofar as it affirms the reality of the individual; it is unacceptable insofar as it defines this reality in terms of substance, as the expression of being understood in itself as truth. The free affirmation is the only passage to reality; outside of this, there can be no question of reality except either in a phenomenal sense or in virtue of the illusion entertained by invincibly abstract and realist thought. The thought of being and being concide (always in the sense of a logic of participation) only in the act by which the individual creates himself. This act is not, however, the magical decree by which the individual becomes the only center; solipsism is an illegitimate solution that is unacceptable from the phenomenal standpoint, as Kant showed, and insufficient from the metaphysical standpoint because the individual is only either a fragment of what in itself is absolute knowledge or a pure form, an empty form. The act that constitutes individuality implies the position of a multiplicity of individualities which it creates—that is, contains the affirmation of an order of love, a level not posited as a world of ideas transcending the sensible world, but implied, as it were, in this particular experience, which real (that is, free) individuality must conceive as constitutive of itself.

B. *Notes on the Problem of Immortality*

The problem of immortality in the religious sense is not absolutely identical with the problem of the soul's survival. Survival might be contingent on a certain system of physical laws of which we are ignorant (transmigration, and so forth). This problem of survival, which is a problem of fact, no more interests religious thought than does the problem of knowing what will be my state of health in twenty years. Could we attempt to give the problem a religious value by making survival (either in its being or in its nature) depend upon the use I shall have made of my freedom? In other words, can we posit transcendental sanctions? But under what conditions are such sanctions conceivable? We must choose between these two alternatives: either the use I will make of my freedom will physically give rise to certain determined effects, or it will be necessary to introduce a being who will seal my destiny in accordance with my merits. Let us examine the first solution: it is evident that an action prolonging itself in knowledge has an indefinite causal effectiveness; but it is not clear whether the consequences of this action must present an ethical character, whether they are subject to a qualification corresponding to the nature of this action. It is obvious that in the sensible no such qualification exists. Now it might be objected that this "obviousness" proves nothing even as regards the sensible order, and especially (the remote repercussions of an act have no importance in relation to the individual destiny) that through death the soul passes into a world where the order of finality replaces that of pure causality. But here the dilemma recurs: Is there some sort of immanent law of development regulating this passage? Or must we introduce the direct regulatory action of some power? The first solution is disastrous to freedom, making it subject to a law of development to which reason would have to submit. It is a return to that old realism in which freedom is an illusion—unless we posit, without trying to reconcile them, individual freedom and the law regulating the distribution of sanctions. This solution is unthinkable and more or less implies the alternative part of the dilemma: the action of divine freedom. Is this freedom conceivable? A superficial analysis of what a sanction is shows that, if it is not a simple reflex accountable to the laws of social physics, then it can only be the thought of a downfall of which we have already spoken. The crass realism which places God before the soul as an exterior judge before a defendant cannot be seriously envisioned. That death by itself is enough to make possible the passage from one world to another would suppose veritable magic or else an absolutely realist and causal concept of grace; once again, death settles nothing in the spiritual sense; and the most distressing problem lies precisely in understanding how an event which is of no interest from a spiritual viewpoint can have significance and a kind of efficaciousness.

We see, then, that this theory of supraterrestrial sanctions is completely devoid of religious significance, and that it presupposes all the ideas which have already been refuted. But the problem remains: How can death be interpreted by thought which participates in being? And is there some internal relation between the uncertainty regarding our salvation (regarding what we are), the uncertainty which is a condition of spiritual progress, and that empirical uncertainty regarding what will happen to us? Here arises again the question which seemed to be set aside but which inevitably reappears, that is, knowing in what sense we can speak of events which are actually unknown and occur after death. We have seen that in any case these events have no relation to how freedom managed itself and can only depend on a certain system of physics which would insure the development of the soul: the soul is here conceived as a substance in a material sense, so to speak, as a passive subject of the modifications which it receives; but we know that freedom is the very negation of this point of view. (To avoid these consequences we would have to return to the idea of a relation between the somehow material destiny of the soul and the use which the soul has made of its freedom.)

Thought participating in being must posit as absolutely foreign and unrelated to what it is essential in itself the modifications which the psychological subject might be capable of undergoing after death.

But then, how can death be conceived by the free mind?

Can we draw any conclusions from the fact that thought cannot conceive itself as annihilated? It is certain that thought cannot grasp itself as annihilated, except by an illusory act, a figment of the imagination which is at the heart of realism. But can it not be objected that thought can grasp the impossibility of conceiving itself as annihilated merely as a subjective condition of its exercise, and can affirm a truth about itself (that of being perishable)? So much so, that, in the final analysis, thought would recognize the necessity of positing its own destruction as an ultimate fact; thus thought would obviously be positing itself (directly or not) as an element and reducing itself to being nothing by itself. Clearly in this sense thought cannot posit itself as mortal, for here again it would forfeit that which is its essential freedom. The psychological impossibility, so to speak, of considering itself as annihilated would be but a symbol of that sort of obligation by which thought cannot, without betraying itself, conceive of itself as something which can be destroyed; and it is clear that this obligation is itself a belief, that faith by which freedom refuses to turn itself into a thing.

Several remarks must be made here. First, this faith bears on personal immortality, in the sense that it is linked to the act of that freedom which is the individual himself in his most profound depth. It is not a matter, then, of an eternity of thought in general; we already know what should be thought of such a notion. We have thus far seen, then, that

freedom cannot posit as transcending itself a fact, a truth
about itself, which would be its mortality. But in that case
the immortality affirmed by faith is not, properly speaking,
a fact. This immortality is not reducible to empirical survival (for nothing related to existence in the empirical sense
can be involved in the order of freedom). Freedom has no
choice but to affirm itself, by faith, a stranger to death, just
as it is alien to time; which merely repeats what we already
know—that death cannot be thought of except as contingent
to one's spiritual development.

But now we seem to be contradicting what was said about
the act by which freedom affirms its relation to experience
to be one of noncontingency. Are we not running the risk of
conceiving freedom as an eternal essence in relation to which
death would only be an unreal accident? Perhaps we can use
here the observation that I cannot think of my death except
as a future event, that I can convert it into an event of the
past only by means of that fiction of which we have already
spoken. Therefore, I can think of my death only by positing
myself as immortal; however, here my death is only fictitious,
and one could maintain that the immortality correlative to
this death is likewise a fictitious immortality. There could
be a real death which would be the insuperable limit of
thought, that which could not be transcended by it. Here
again freedom would be shattered against the rampart of
fact. To avoid this, it suffices to remark that this real death
is precisely nonbeing (it is the exact equivalent of the thing-

in-itself of realism). It becomes more and more clear that the thought of death can only appear to reflection as a pure fiction. It might be objected that my death can be truly thought of by others; but it is obvious that that which can be thought of by others is in no way my death in the sense which is here in question. It is a physical event; to place the truth of myself in the thought of others is to make of myself a notion, an essence—it is to deny all which has laboriously affirmed up until now. For faith, that is, for thought which has overcome the abstract and the imaginary, *there is no death:* "O Death, where is thy sting?"

But are we now led to the very denial of the problems of death? Clearly such a denial would be radically superficial. The positing of death as a problem is implicit in the act of love, that is, love wills its object as transcending death, not as an eternal essence, but as surviving death. Love implies the affirmation of survival (and we must affirm ourselves as surviving, to the extent that we are objects of love). Love does not create survival, but it does involve its affirmation. Will someone object that this survival can only be an afterlife in thought, in memory? Well, this afterlife must appear only as the symbol, as the psychological transposition, of a true afterlife. It is in this sense that love vanquishes death; it negates death. Will someone object that this "true survival" remains empirical and in fact forms a part of the order of truth, of the verifiable order, that it can be false? But it must be absolutely denied that any verification is possible. Death withdraws the individual from the order of verification, of possible experience—and it is in this sense that affirmation of a real afterlife cannot be false. It will be objected that this comes down to denying the possibility of nonperceptual, nonphysical experience. In answer it must be said that the Kantian critique of mysticism, of internal experience, is still valid; and it would seem that (either in a Kantian or a Leibnizian sense) the subject of an experience can only look at itself objectively if it posits itself as a spatial datum, as a body. The affirmation of an afterlife is therefore linked to love, and cannot be separated from it; as soon as survival is posited as an objective fact, it becomes a pure figment of the imagination which has nothing to do with metaphysics.

It is understandable, then, why we can say that immortality is a belief, if faith is, of its very essence, an act which does not allow itself to be subjected to any possible verification. It is clear also why immortality thus defined can be neither imagined nor represented on a level of transcendent experience (which is contradictory).

A number of difficulties arise at this point. It can be objected that empirically love can be reconcilable with the belief in annihilation. But we already know what answer must be given: we are dealing with the right of a free mind; no doubt it can give up these rights; but by such abdication it renounces being free in its own eyes, it prostrates itself before the idol of a physical truth.

On the other hand, one might well ask what the meaning

of real afterlife is. It must be answered, it seems, that for the mind which affirms it this survival is posited as not a mere ideal survival; the reality of survival is as yet defined only in a negative manner; thought affirms survival as distinct from the idea which it has of survival; and thought affirms survival as an object. But then do we not fall back into the order of experience and of verification? Are we not dealing with a belief which bears upon fact, and can thereby be true or false? Survival thus affirmed seems to possess the contradictory characteristics of being a truth and at the same time transcending all verification.[20] The reality of survival, it seems, can only be its action, and in this sense there is room for a practical verification, which is the action in us of what survives; this action must not appear as a mere reflection, as a mere subjective prolongation of this real afterlife, but the expression of it, an idea which is negated as pure idea, and which embodies in itself the power of faith to make things real. Real afterlife then must be conceived as a symbol which thought owes itself not to think of as symbol; it is what freedom imagines—an image which has the characteristic of not having to be conceived as fiction.

"Evasions!" some will maintain. Is the afterlife an objective reality, or is it only a transposition of subjective needs, of mere psychological data? All our work leads us to reject the

[20] The impossibility of verification is basically not of the empirical order; it is essentially linked to the relation which joins the affirmation of survival to love, and which makes a belief of this affirmation.

dilemma; for it always presupposes the identification of being with truth, and we have rejected this identification from
the first. In a word the psychological, the subjective, is posited as relative to an objective truth which is considered the
last obstacle which thought meets, before which it comes to
a halt. And from the standpoint of truth (and of a "realism
of the true") we must agree that it is indeed so; and it is because of this that the very notion of the psychological is a
well-founded notion. Only for thought which has raised itself to the level of freedom does this dilemma cease to be
valid; the dilemma is significant only within determined
limits, which are those of the level of objects, of what can
be called the world of ideas. By virtue of its own power, an
act transcends this world of ideas, denying it as an ultimate.
But it is precisely in terms of an act (specifying itself in love)
that faith in immortality must be conceived.

We can now see in what sense there is a problem of immortality even for myself and how obscure this problem is.
For my immortality cannot be thought directly by me. I can
think of myself as immortal only insofar as I am myself the
creation of an act of love. It might be objected that this
comes down to saying: *I can think of myself as immortal
only in the loving thought of others.* This conclusion, however, is utterly false. Such a solution is contradictory and
useless, because the afterlife which is an object of faith involves an act of transcendence which negates what, to reflection, appears as its own subjective conditions of elabora-

tion (or rather, that which posits these as contingent). Thus
it seems that my faith in my own immortality has a bearing
upon the identity of the individuality which I create in myself and upon this creation of love whose survival others will
affirm by faith. It must be acknowledged that this solution
is obscure; furthermore, it presents the difficulty that faith
in immortality seems linked to the fact that others will sur-
vive my death, and this empirical fact can only be contingent.
But what of it? What we must do is to go beyond the still
relatively empirical order in which we have, until now, been
moving. That is, no doubt we cannot subordinate the possibility of our being objects of love to the existence of empirical data (of other individual minds).[21] And thus it seems
that love, as the higher life of thought, is built on new bases,
insofar as I can think of myself as able to become an object
of love for God. God could then be defined as the keystone
of the kingdom of love. And everything that has previously
been said about the acts by which individual minds affirm
one another as immortal would, from this new point of view,
merely symbolize the living communication of the individual
with God. This communication, as we already know, is participation. We know that it is not mere knowledge, and that
it ceases as soon as the individual mind, seeking to free itself
from God, claims to posit Him before itself as a being; we
love only insofar as we do not try to know. Love is always a

[21] From the new viewpoint which we have now reached, these
would appear to be only mediators.

belief. The supreme truth of the myth of Psyche is precisely that thought, when seeking to determine the content of love, ceases to be free. All this we knew already; but what we discover, it seems, is that thought affirms, as it were, the possibility of an ineffable echo in God, of an act by which God re-creates it in love, and by a bold and creative transposition individuality somehow takes possession again of that which it had seemed to abandon as alien to its essential nature and posits itself as a creature (by the act which posits the noncontingency of its particular experience). A true spiritual life begins only with the affirmation of a reciprocity in God, of a response, and this affirmation is prayer.

C. Notes on the Unverifiable

The act which posits the noncontingency of the relation between formal thought and its empirical content is the equivalent of the monad. Instead of positing this relation as the truth implied in the system of essences, it is here affirmed by an act which transcends all possible knowing. By this act, the individual constitutes itself as such (but in the least substantialist sense possible).

A truth can only be thought of as the relation between conceptual thought and sensible intuition (this, obviously, is the most basic result of critical philosophy); in this sense it could be said that a truth cannot be posited outside a relation to sensible experience. Basically, a truth is the intelligible content of an experience, insofar as this content is revealed to conceptual thought. The latter necessarily tends to isolate this content and to treat as contingent the experience which furnishes it, and in this way, leads to a rationalism which is *in se* Platonic; by way of reaction, empiricism posits this experience as a reality, arbitrarily isolating it without seeing that, in doing so, either it converts it into an idea (and this leads to pure Idealism), or it does not conceptualize it at all. The solution consists in positing the relation to experience as the constitutive element of a particular truth (herein lies the contributions of critical philosophy), that is, in not positing a truth as transcending all verification, on the contrary, in understanding as essential the immanent bond uniting truth to verification.

Only from this viewpoint does thought for which truth is possible appear as an essentially limited order; and, thereby, a philosophy which would identify the true with the real reveals its narrowness and its insufficiency. The soul of truth is not this purely apparent intelligible kernel to which being would be reduced, but rather verifying thought, or better, the synthetic act which links a system of affirmations—a rational system—to experience which is posited as a condition. It might be objected that experience remains a constitutive element of truth and that it is not defined; however, it must doubtlessly be said in answer that to those who were to try to strip from experience the veil of sensible appearances, the experience would reveal itself identical with the very movement of consciousness (delve into this further).

What is essential is that the transposition of the notion of truth to the order in which verification is impossible is illusory and unlawful; there is no historical truth except in the sense that there is an act of historical imagination, symbolizing the sensible and temporal intuition of the past; and there is not and cannot be a truth of religious history, or at least this truth can be reduced to no more than the representation of the most immediate forms of religion. The scientific study of religion consequently excludes, by definition, all that is not pure morphology; and the nihilistic conclusions to which it leads are essentially implied in its very notion. There is a truth only of that which, at least in the ideal order, can become actual once again, that is, become once again an object of experience for me, and for me insofar as I am thought-in-general. For me, religion cannot turn into this—that would be its very negation, and it would dissolve in this case into a pure fabrication.

Basic to all this is the notion of the unverifiable—the problem of knowing how an unverifiable can be nonfictional. Freedom is the model of this kind of unverifiable; it is the unverifiable *par excellence*, and if it were otherwise, freedom would be a physical cause. Reality cannot but be unverifiable; and it is in this sense that a miracle can be real, not because it is a truth (for as physical, as an experience, a miracle is impossible), but because it is unverifiable, that is, linked to an awareness which it is by definition unable to reconstitute as an event. In this sense, there is no possible critique of a miracle, for such a critique would destroy only an abstraction; and such an abstraction is not the miracle.

IV

Theory of Participation, 1913-1914

[*Manuscript XVIII*]

The fundamental propositions of the theory of participation seem to be the following: first, participation is not a fact, not a dictum of the mind; it is a demand of free thought, a demand which is fulfilled by the very act of positing it, since its fulfillment depends on no condition external to itself. We can, however, distinguish two stages in participation, depending on whether it is defined as an object of thought, or as thought, renouncing its function as a thinking subject, which abandons itself entirely to participation; this second stage alone deserves to be called faith. In a certain sense, faith is more than an immanent act, since it is the crowning point of a dialectic entirely oriented towards transcendence. Furthermore, it is clear (and this is how its transcendence is defined) that this faith can in no wise become explicit in a judgment, because the subject which posits an existential judgment is thought caught up in becoming, thought engaged in a world of affirmations which do not become explicit to it; and faith, on the contrary, is the very essence of freedom. Faith, then, is not affirming that something exists; the problem of God's existence, a problem absolutely devoid of metaphysical significance, would never have been raised had it not been for a crass intellectualism which remained prisoner of empirical thought's contingent modes of positing. Maimonides was right in saying that existence is an unsuitable concept to apply to God. Nor is faith the positing of an essence—this is evident. Faith, in short, can only be defined in relation to the dialectical movement of which it is the culmination.

Faith cannot be known, but it can be the object of thought —for thought which has triumphed over knowing (*Trieb zum Wissem*) thinks itself as transcendent in relation to knowledge. It can further be said that faith bears upon a certain life of thought which it creates by its very exercise and which consequently cannot be conceived as pre-existent to thought-life. The profound idea of a spiritual rebirth (*Wiedergeburt*) is thus basically well founded. Faith is all at once a death and a birth: it is birth to this life of thought (which is not intellectual and which is religion) and death with regard to that order of knowing in which thought can conceive itself only as object, almost, we might say, as thing. It would not be permissible then to ask if faith is a real communication with a being distant from us; for this would be posing the problem in terms in which it can neither be re-

solved, nor even present a meaning. Faith creates individuality, and individuality is thought participating in being. It
might be added that faith is the more manifest, the more it
does not limit itself to the sphere of what is empirically called
individuality; for, from the point of view of faith, the distinction into individual spheres (in the psychological sense) is
meaningless. That is why prayer, that is, the essential act of
faith, cannot help bearing upon the salvation of others. Thus
the act of faith clearly cannot be conceived as the act of an
empirical subject, for, in thus considering it, we would be
maintaining to know it (to determine it, be it in the manner
of a fetish as a relation between one being and another, or
psychologically as auto-suggestion). And we know that there
cannot be between the thought of faith and faith itself a
distinction such as that which exists between knowledge and
the object known; rather, the thought of faith is faith being
born—faith, as it were, newly sown. This is another way of
saying that faith is conceivable in its being only *for itself*,
only in relation to itself as itself (not as this or that kind of
being). Besides the truth of the self (which is to be this kind
of person or that), there is a reality of the self (as pure self)
which can appear explicitly only through faith in that it is
demanded by faith. To conceive the faith of another is really
not to conceive it, not to consider anything at all; and to
conceive faith for oneself is possible only under condition of
eliminating from this "self" (by an ideal transposition of self
into another psychological context) whatever could be re-

garded as "other." And to the objection that the self thus extended could only be a form, it suffices to answer that thought only appears to itself as form when it illegitimately converts into an object that which, in itself, is pure subjectivity. The preceding remarks allow us to distinguish a superficial subjectivism which identifies individuality with what it is as an object of knowledge and for which there are faiths and religions—from a profound subjectivism for which faith finds no support except in the *self* and there is only *faith* and religion. We could say that the formal unicity of the *ego* is only the translation, on the level of reflexive knowledge, of the substantial unicity of the self.

The *self* might well be (negatively) characterized if we said that it is nothing which can be found (which is given), for on reflecting on myself, I find only an empty form or an empirical content; but neither the one nor the other can be the subject of faith. This concrete reality must be an act. But upon what can this act bear? It can only be upon the act of creation, the act of active knowledge of the *ego* by which the *self* enters a state of becoming, and this act is broadly defined as love. The subject of faith can only be individuality which affirms itself in love and cannot exist outside of it. Love, far from being the product of faith, as a superficial analysis might lead us to believe, is a necessary condition for it.

Essentially, love is the act of a free mind affirming another free self and which is free only by this very affirmation. There is, at the root of love, the belief in the inexhaustible richness

and the unpredictable spontaneity of the being who is loved.
From the moment when this being is posited as an object,
love becomes knowledge, and the creative freedom of the
lover becomes fettered and transformed into an abstract
form which will soon allow the reappearance of that abstract
content which is the empirical individuality. Thought, then,
is love insofar as it is creative interpretation—and in this
measure it is also pure freedom. Love cannot be an object of
knowledge, for the individuality which is actualized in love
goes beyond knowledge, and transcends it then and there.
And love is not a game of subjective illusions, for there is no
subjectivity, in the exact sense of that term, except in opposition to the objectivity of an abstract knowing. We participate in being, therefore, only in the measure that we
make ourselves individuals, that we create ourselves through
love as pure subjects. But is love this participation itself? Is
love this life in God to which one must be born anew in order
to have true being? Or is it only an introduction or a prelude
to it?

Before we discuss this question, let us see how the problem of the metaphysical basis of love is posed and, if necessary, how it is resolved. The problem obviously arises because
love, without, properly speaking, being an essence, is a thinking mind, in the deepest sense of the word an intelligible (an
intelligible movement of the mind—perhaps the very acts
by which mind becomes mind). From all that has preceded,
it follows that this basis does not reside in an objective shar-

ing in a common element. Love does not express the community of nature of individual minds—and it is not grounded on the fact that these minds participate in the same essence. If then we maintain, as we doubtlessly must, that love has a religious basis, it will not be in the sense that creatures are in communion through their participation in the divine perfections. For a new problem would arise, that of knowing why these divine perfections are themselves objects of love, and we would be unable to close the discussion except by seeing in love the subjective echo of intellection—and we already know what must be thought of such a theory. Certainly, there is a community of nature between individual thinking minds, but only in the measure that one individual can be an object of knowledge for another individual; but we know that love is beyond such truth. There is thus no objective basis for love. To think otherwise is to intellectualize it, to fall back into the metaphysics of pure knowing. It must be acknowledged, if necessary, that love expresses nothing, and that therein lies its basic originality.[22]

We must give up believing that when we love we see things or beings such as they are in themselves, in the sense that love would be the most perfect approximation of the truth of these beings, and, as it were, an imitation of an adequate knowledge. *Love can only be given a basis as an act*; to justify it objectively is to negate it, purely and simply.

[22] Perhaps this is profoundly true of art also, and thus the deep relationship between art and love becomes clear.

Strictly speaking, then, no being is worthy of being loved, if by worthiness is meant something which would objectively draw love to itself: merit. Love is always necessarily a grace; the order of love is beyond the relative world of merit and demerit (which depend upon collective purposes)—it is the order of the free gift. Nor is it a world; whereas the sphere of ethical relations, in affirming itself, necessarily tends to become totalized in a system, the order of grace would negate itself in becoming a world;[23] and the arbitrary is only the reverse side of the metaphysical (considered in its relation to ethics, that is, to the abstract).[24]

If, then, it can be said that all love is in God, it is not in the sense that all love in some confused way involves perfectly adequate knowledge, but in the sense that all love is the dynamic motion of a free mind which *has being* only if its fulcrum is outside of itself, that is, if it creates. Love then is not being, nor is it a revelation of being either. If love in any way is an objective revelation, it is not the act by which perfections are made manifest to us; love could be revelation only because it would allow thought to discover in itself the creative spontaneity which is there. But here again the road leading to faith is strewn with stumbling blocks, for if the

[23] Herein lies the whole difference between democratic morality which is but that, and Christian morality which is more than an ethical system. [Word "morale" is missing in the French, after "qu'une."]

[24] One should mention here the two orders so vaguely distinguished by Bergson.

individual mind appears to itself as being the real center of projection around which are deployed the fabrications of love, if love appears to itself as a marvelous spectacle which individuality has provided for itself, then this individuality falls back into the world of knowledge, into the world of empirical flux where reigns the dualism of the apparent and the real—it negates itself. Are we not then led to the conclusion that individuality *has being* only under condition of deceiving itself and of enclosing itself into an unthinking illusionism? But at this point, the problem cannot and should not arise in these terms. True illusionism, the only illusionism which deserves the name, is that which closes its eyes voluntarily to a truth, which calls truth that which is error, or vice-versa; for the object of knowledge is necessarily posited as that in relation to which the qualifications which we attribute to it are contingent. Here this is not the case, and between the interpretation and the thing interpreted there is no real dualism, or rather this dualism cannot be an object of knowledge; to affirm it is to make it have being, to create it. Truly free thought must forbid itself the consideration of love as illusion, for there is nothing, we know, which can be the truth of love, nothing to which love can be what an illusion is to a truth. Thought must know how to resist the temptation to consider love as knowledge, or as illusion; for thought, by giving in to it, would once again negate itself as freedom. Now, at this point, there are no perils for thought except those which threaten its freedom. Beyond love there is thus the act which affirms love as real, as incommensurable with any truth whatever, because it is not knowledge. This act is free—it is a belief, it is faith.

Yet, what precedes immediately obliges us to clear up a new ambiguity to which these conclusions inevitably give rise. It would be wrong to infer from what has been said that God ought to be, or even could be, determined, directly at least, as love. Such an inference would be either saying nothing precise, or objectivizing that which appears to unreflective thought as the deep communication of substances, and the truth of which we have seen resides in a free act. And thus is resolved the question of the relation between being and love which was brought up at the beginning. All we can say is that, to the free mind which refuses to treat it as a confused knowledge, love appears as being in the line of being. Insofar as all values correspond to free acts and arrange themselves into a hierarchy just as do the acts themselves, we can thus say that love is a superior value (which does not permit the transposition of this value into the ontological order).

Perhaps a more profound analysis of participation will allow us to grasp more deeply the very problem of the divine. The highest act which we have reached is that which affirms the reality of love as transcending all possible knowledge. But what is the relation involved in this act, between love itself and the object loved? We have negatively determined this relation by saying that love does not express the nature of the object, that this nature is not itself truth, since its proper character is not to have any truth (which also excludes the naïve subjectivism according to which love is supposed to express the psychological nature of the lover). Need we conclude that, from the point of view which we have reached, the nature of the object, the object as object, must necessarily appear radically contingent in relation to the act of love itself, which would permit a passage to the notion of an abstract love which would be the highest stage of the practical dialectic? The answer seems to be this: In opposing the reality of an abstract love to the contingent forms which it would put on, an analogous, if not identical, dualism is re-established with that of the true and the false; there would be reinstated the realist opposition between that which is and that which is only in appearance or, more exactly, between that which is essentially and that which is only accidentally. But that this distinction has a validity of capital importance in the order of knowing is most probably what must be acknowledged; we must no doubt deny that here the distinction has any meaning, for, at the point we have reached, we could not reintroduce the opposition between the abstract and the concrete (especially in favor of the abstract) without contradicting the fundamental data of the theory of participation. It is not, then, accidental that love bears upon a certain determined content, in the sense that the notion of contingency is here devoid of all meaning. This comes down to saying that there would be no possible truth of an af-

firmation about the contingent character of the object in
relation to love. Or again, thought affirms itself as truly free
only in the measure in which it forbids itself to judge the
object as contingent in relation to the movement which di-
rects it toward that object. But this is clearly valid in a general way for whatever is given to thought as experience; experience appears to thought as contingent to it only in the
measure in which thought defines itself as a form and an
abstraction. Insofar as thought thinks and desires itself as
free,[25] the particular experiences to which it is bound must
seem to be in spiritual relation to it, to have to be conceived
as *willed*,[26] and thus, for the first time in the dialectic, appears the affirmation of a will, of a divine freedom, which
alone can account for the relation which the free mind estab-
lishes between itself and experience. It is not necessary to
repeat that this act of willing is not an object, and that it
can in no way be considered such. This is aptly expressed by
the idea that the ways of God are impenetrable; that is, the
impossibility, the invalidity, of such an objectivization is
expressed by us by supposing a transcendent knowledge
which supports this will and which it intends to actualize.[27]

What, then, is essential in the affirmation of a divine will

[25] There lies, it seems to me, the profound meaning of the "yes"
which Nietzsche's superman gives to life.
[26] Or again in the most powerful and concrete meaning of the
word, as *given*.
[27] But this solution is contradictory in that it re-establishes in God
the dualism of matter and form.

is the act by which free thought postulates a transcendental relation between itself and a reality (in the empirical sense of that term) which must be accepted. By the act of faith the free mind refuses definitively either to cut itself off, in sterile solitude, from an experience which it is, of itself, incapable of deducing, or to identify itself with this experience in order to make itself fit into the entirety of knowledge. And free thought gives birth to itself as individual by relating itself to a will which it is obliged to affirm as free or as concrete under pain of negating itself—and this by an act which would itself be free, and consequently contradictory, by an act which would be sin itself if it is true that sin is the act of a free mind denying that it is free.

Thus we reach the apparently paradoxical conclusion that a free individual cannot be defined except in relation to a divine freedom, and by considering the world as a product of this freedom. The thesis to which we are led is not at all the one according to which freedom would be a necessity which is accepted; for this is only valid for an intellectualism which places individuality in participation in reason, and we already know why this position is untenable.

A few remarks will give precision to the position which we are espousing. First, the divine will is not an object, that is, we cannot claim to read it, to grasp it through certain objective signs—to judge it otherwise would be to fall into a veritable fetishism. And it is for this reason that the divine will must cease to have being in any way for whoever denies it in thought or in action, because it is not a power, an objective datum which imposes itself upon consciousness. It must again be repeated: the divine freedom can only be affirmed or denied freely, only by a mind; and in this metaphysical sense the power of free choice cannot be denied (in fact, the denial of free choice actually presupposes it). There is then nothing in thought which is not freedom, but there can be different degrees of freedom; there is the free mind which does not know itself, and in so doing negates itself, and we have already said that it is the root of evil; there is a free mind which affirms itself and wills itself, and we know that this freedom can only be that faith in a God which links it to the world. Consequently, it is in my power to be or not to be, for I shall be only by thinking and willing my being, by having faith in it; and I will be able to conceive my being (since I am nothing either as form or as empirical content) only by affirming that I have been willed and created, and that the universe has been willed and created along with me. To think oneself free and at the same time willed is far from being contradictory, as a superficial philosophy would tend to have us believe. Each of these two affirmations, strictly speaking, is possible only if the other is affirmed. And this becomes immediately clear if we consider that we can only be willed as free, that what is willed in us can only be freedom. We know as a matter of fact that we are forbidden to attribute to the divine will any sort of objective content, for this would reintroduce the chimera of transcendental knowl-

edge and would be in absolute contradiction to the first principles of the philosophy of participation. And this is not opposed to what has already been said, for we must not forget
that it is the relation of thought to experience which must
appear as rooted in God—this being a belief, being faith.[28]
It thus seems to be at the root of the free act that faith
necessarily appears. This, it seems, can be made more precise.
The free act necessarily bears upon the empirical content of
thought, and we already know that it would be contrary to
its very essence to distinguish in it a pure form and a contingent matter. Thought will affirm itself as free only by
affirming a willed relation between itself (as subject, not as
form) and this matter. It is possible that thought might go
beyond this conclusion, which is metaphysically well
founded, and go so far as to believe itself to be the instru-
ment of the divine will's realization. But it does not seem
that in this belief we can see anything but an illusion, for it
presupposes a knowledge of the divine will which would reduce it to being only an object or a system of knowledge
(which naturally comes to the same thing anyway).[29] By

[28] It is upon this relation that faith in God as Creator bears; this
faith in no way implies—and it probably even excludes as being of
another order and purely mythical—the idea of a systematic knowledge of creation or a sort of divine history of the world. Or again,
faith bears necessarily and essentially upon the present (which is the
temporal *locus* of the act).

[29] However a problem arises here: This free act makes possible the
matter of new free acts; this matter will be the datum which these

right, thought must appear to itself as willed only insofar as
it is free and insofar as this freedom requires infinite conditions for its exercise; the act itself excludes every conceivable
relation with God. We must therefore reject all the simplistic
interpretations according to which the individual ought to
tend to make himself God's collaborator. The world cannot
be considered created, except insofar as it is the mass of conditions for free action. It could be said without exaggeration
that the freely acting individual is in a sense (must appear as
being) the end, the goal, of creation. Nevertheless, it is clear
that such a mode of expression would lend itself to very
serious equivocations, and that the legitimacy of any affirmation bearing upon a transcendent finality, of any objective
determination of the content of the divine work, must be
denied. For this work would be posited as truth belonging
to the world, as a true content—and we already know why
such a position cannot be metaphysically valid.[30]

There is, then, a most intimate link between the free act

---

acts will meet; and hence this matter will also have to be considered
as willed. Thus is explained the illusion according to which freedom
itself is an illusion and enters into a pre-established order. But this
conclusion, untenable in itself and ruining essentially the notion of
individuality, can be avoided by positing the absolute discontinuity
of free acts which can be related to each other only from a phe-
nomenological point of view (and insofar as they are considered as
stages of knowledge).

[30] The contradiction could easily be expressed thus: the divine
work exists only for him who participates in it; and participating in
the divine work excludes positing it as object.

and the affirmation of the divine will. It might even be said that we participate in God only in the measure in which we act freely; but here again we must be careful about inexact interpretations. We well know that the free act is not the true act, the act which embodies the divine causality; and for us, participation must actually be understood in a radically different sense. But we must notice that, properly speaking, the problem of participation is made singularly obscure by the fundamental ambiguity of the notion of freedom. We have spoken of a free act but, strictly speaking, every act is free; however, this freedom, as we have seen, can consist in negating itself as such. And in this sense it could be said that even the concrete negation of God (that is, the action which cancels itself out as an action), a denial which is transcendentally possible only for God himself, involves and encompasses the affirmation of divine freedom. But let us be careful: we have said that freedom does not exist for itself, cannot be conceived of as freedom, except by affirming that its relation to experience is founded on God. This affirmation is faith, that is, participation itself. But since participation is not a truth, it cannot be affirmed without contradiction by one who does not affirm it.

It is important to look back and make even more precise what must be conceived as willed by God. Have we not in effect imprudently identified the freedom of which we were treating with what in the temporal order presents itself as an act? In a word, is there not at the heart of the very notion

of the actual an equivocation which should be cleared up?
Every effort must then be brought to bear upon the starting
point of these new investigations, that is, the noncontingency of individuality's empirical content. We know that
this noncontingency must be affirmed by the free mind if
the latter wishes to be (that is, to have an individual being),
that the free mind, consequently, is not (we shall say does
not participate in being) except by thinking a divine will
establishing a spiritual relation between it and its content.
Thus, there is an act by which another act is affirmed. This
faith is defined from our point of view as the act of a free
mind which postulates a divine act to understand itself, and,
strictly speaking, to make itself possible, postulates a divine
act. (What is paradoxical and even contradictory in this
formulation allows us to grasp well the antinomic character
of faith.)

But this empirical content cannot, without contradiction,
be regarded as pure instantaneity, as the slice of experience,
so to speak, concomitant with the act of faith. For this act is
not really temporal; it is temporal only for psychological reflection, which situates and orders it in relation to empirical
becoming. Faith[31] then bears upon the relation between
thought and experience as a whole (in the past as well as in
the future), in its indivisible and yet complex unity. Every
action, if we take the word in its strongest and most concrete

[31] By faith I conceive my experience, my very life, as an act of
God.

sense, requires this faith without which it could be conceived only as a mechanism or as the contingent exercise of a formal reasoning power without any relation to the world to which it applies. Action presupposes faith and, on the other hand, faith which does not lead to action runs the risk of degenerating into that contradictory knowledge which is mysticism, that is, that intuition which does not grasp itself as creative and relies upon an illusory objectivity.

But, it might be objected, this nontemporal act of faith nonetheless unfolds itself in distinct temporal actions, to which must nevertheless correspond acts of faith which are themselves distinct. Maybe we should answer that the plurality of these acts is not metaphysically any more thinkable than the plurality of consciousness, that is, it is thinkable only for a reflecting mind which orders these acts into a becoming exterior to itself, a mind which therefore sacrifices what is still freedom in favor of the empirical matter in which it is submerged. We could express this by saying that the free act can appear as a unit among other units, as a unit of a series, only insofar as it manifests a nature; but we know that the proper nature of free thought is to be more than a nature, and we can understand from this point of view that action, properly so called, is essentially something which cannot be made to fit into a web of this sort.[32]

---

[32] In a word, just as consciousnesses cannot be thought of as expressions of the same essence, as representations, insofar as they are consciousnesses, of the same truth, so also free acts, as free, cannot

And the aforementioned difficulty (about the necessity
seemingly arising out of our position of conceiving the act,
after it has taken place, as the divine volition, as the very act
of God) arises, no doubt, because the problem[33] was presented in contradictory terms, because by free act was understood an exterior movement of the mind (that is, the mind
going outside itself vis-à-vis immediate consciousness). Up to
now, all we know is faith, that is, the act by which thought affirms the noncontingency of its relation to experience; at this
point, it seems that an act, generally speaking, is free in the
measure in which it includes this affirmation (which itself
basically requires the identification of the eternal with the
actual), that is, it is free through what is nonhistorical in it.
But have we not reached a point where we are dissecting individual becoming, in the sense that seemingly we cannot
situate the free act, as free, within a development? At this
point of the discussion, it seems then that the becoming of
the individual is essentially unintelligible and unthinkable.
Could we not express this by saying that there is no possible
reconciliation between thought about the dialectical development and the thought which affirms freedom? But then

---

be emanations of one identical volition; but it is precisely insofar as
they are consciousnesses that they cannot be thought of as many,
and we could say equally that insofar as they are free, the acts cannot
be thought as many.

[33] It now becomes clear, as Leibniz saw, that the problem of the
relation between the one and the many is the fundamental problem
of philosophy.

are we not back to the Kantian dualism of the noumenal world and the empirical world? It is easy to see the danger which would arise in re-establishing this dualism, and that this re-establishment would only be the imperfect and ambiguous transposition of all the conclusions which have been already reached.

In reality, the free act cannot be posited as an object without contradiction. The free act, for reflection, is not; it has being only for reflection which negates itself (that is, for freedom); freedom or faith cannot therefore be ordered in relation to a world of objects (empirical becoming), that is, between the one and the other no relation is conceivable. Freedom (that is, thought grasping itself in the actual order) is the pure and simple negation of any element of the past (in this sense, and only in this sense, can we talk of an absolute beginning). If now it is said that this negation is illusory, it can only be in the name of a psychical substantialism underlying the affirmations of a permanent subject, an essence which would manifest itself in the act. But we already know that a free act is nothing of the sort, that reflection alone strains to interpret the act in this way in order to find the truth of it (that is, to negate it as free), and that this would be valid only in absolute Idealism; furthermore, this reflection itself would be an act, of which there is no truth (a contradictory act).

Postface (Epilogue)

When the editor asked me if I would not write a brief epilogue to the text the reader has just perused, my first reaction was to refuse. While correcting the proofs, I had many times become exasperated by the *lacunae*, or even the contradictions, which I found in these writings of my youth.

But a recent meeting has somewhat changed my disposition. I have had the good fortune in the last few days of seeing, after many years, a man who seems to me to be one of the most authentic of God's witnesses whom I have had the good fortune of knowing during my life. I am speaking of Marcel Legaut, the author of *The Christian Condition*, that mathematician who in 1940, after the disaster, went to live with a few friends in a hamlet lost in the mountains of the Drôme, where he now leads the life of a contemplative shepherd. In that austere and magnificent place, he lives in God's presence. I had met him for the first time in 1935, that is, long after having written the essays which appear in this little book. But it is certain that he gave me an astonishing confirmation of the existential assurance around which these writings gravitate. I am referring to the unimpeachable character of faith when it is perfectly authentic. What is unique is that this character impressed itself upon me at a time when in all honesty I could not yet consider myself as a believer. Here is, it seems to me, the *paradox* which lends some significance to these texts and which permits us to consider them as *existential by anticipation*, although the word still does not appear anywhere in these pages.

If I ask myself how this assurance, indeed very mysterious, took hold of me, I think I can say that it is through *music* and particularly through the cantatas and Passions of Johann Sebastian Bach that it came both into my heart and into my mind, without, moreover, my feeling at that time the need of asking by what means this mediation was taking place. At that time my attention was polarized, so to speak, by the reality whose witness was thus presented to me.

Thus we find recurring the inevitably spiral character of that intellectual motion which is one of the constants of my mind.

Les Ollières

Da